...AND THE ANGELS CAME

Dr. Larry Brothers

ISBN (eBook): 979-8-218-21409-8
ISBN (Print): 979-8-218-21895-9

For inquiries write andtheangelscame@gmail.com
or visit www.andtheangelscame.com

I would like to dedicate this book to:

*Honor the One Who ordained this project and directed my
steps, and is faithful to His Word.
To my wife, Rosie, son, Dalton, and his wife, Christa.
To our three beautiful granddaughters.
And to the people of Joplin and Duquesne, Missouri.*

CONTENTS

FOREWORD

"For He shall give His angels charge over you,
to keep you in all your ways.
In their hands they shall bear you up, lest you
dash your foot against a stone.
You shall tread upon the lion and the cobra,
the young lion and the serpent you shall trample underfoot.

"'Because he has set his love upon Me, therefore I will deliver him;
I will set him on high, because he has known My name.
He shall call upon Me, and I will answer him;
I will be with him in trouble;
I will deliver him and honor him.'"
Psalm 91:11-15 (NKJV)

The Lord Jesus is our deliverer, and He is the Word who became flesh! Yeshua, Jesus has charge of all those who call on the name of the Lord.

"...And the Angels Came" is a testimonial record and beautiful evidence of angels ministering mercy and grace to those experiencing a time of most intense need. When there is no explanation, when loss is all consuming, when hope is flickering, and when there are no answers... no words... God answers us with supernatural deliverance in our times of trouble.

Perhaps you are reading this book because have never had an angelic encounter. Maybe you have even wondered if angels truly exist. Or perhaps you viewed angels as smiling, chubby cherubs.

"…And the Angels Came" gives us an opportunity to see angels on a personal and powerful level and gain understanding on their divine interaction with our lives. We have an opportunity to see what God says about His messengers:

Angels are responsible to perform the Word of God and carry out His promises in your life…

"Bless the Lord, you His angels,
who excel in strength, who do His word,
heeding the voice of His word.
Bless the Lord, all you His hosts,
You ministers of His, who do His pleasure.
Bless the Lord, all His works,
in all places of His dominion.

"Bless the Lord, O my soul!"
Psalm 103:20-22 (NKJV)

Angels ministered to Jesus and are still ministering to His followers today…

"And He was there in the wilderness forty days, tempted
by Satan, and was with the wild beasts;
and the angels ministered to Him."
Mark 1:13 (NKJV)

"Likewise, I say to you, there is joy in the presence of
the angels of God over one sinner who repents."
Luke 15:10 (NKJV)

Angels are part of end-time ministry…

"So it will be at the end of the age.
The angels will come forth, separate the
wicked from among the just…"
Matthew 13:49 (NKJV)

Jesus gave His angels charge over you...

*"For it is written: 'He shall give His angels
charge over you, to keep you...'"*
Luke 4:10 (NKJV)

Regardless, of what you know, understand, or believe about angelic hosts, *"...And the Angels Came"* does an incredible job of sharing hidden treasures that were found and birthed through tragedy. You will be transformed in your faith as you read testimonies about the faithfulness of God's Word and His powerful angelic army.

The words and the testimonies within *"...And the Angels Came"* will bring you peace and remind you that you are not alone, and that God truly cares for His creation! Our God is love and His angels are ministers of love that bring comfort, protection, and peace—sometimes invisibly and sometimes when our spiritual eyes are wide-open.

*"But to which of the angels has He ever said:
'Sit at My right hand, till I make Your enemies Your footstool'?
Are they not all ministering spirits sent forth to
minister for those who will inherit salvation?*
Hebrews 1:13-14 (NKJV)

Foreword by: Curt Landry, Founder
Curt Landry Ministries
www.CurtLandry.com

INTRODUCTION

The events that took place on the afternoon of Sunday, May 22, 2011, in the cities of Joplin and Duquesne, Missouri changed the lives of the people of those communities forever. The cities would be the setting for the development of an EF-5 tornado. In reference to the casualties that resulted, this particular storm was rated as the seventh-largest single tornado in the United States. It was the largest tornado to strike the United States in approximately 60 years.

This monster of a storm touched down near the western city limits of Joplin that afternoon and moved slowly across the middle section of the city, destroying almost everything in its path. The storm would eventually retreat into the clouds nearly 20 miles to the east, about a half hour later. At times, the width of damage stretched out as far as 1 mile from the center line of the path through the city. This storm resulted in the destruction or near destruction of 6,000 to 8,000 buildings. A survey of nearly 2,000 people questioned in the months following the storm revealed that more than 35 percent of people who lived within the city of Joplin had been displaced from their homes due to the storm—more than one-third of the people of Joplin had essentially been rendered homeless. There were approximately 550 businesses that were severely damaged or totally destroyed. This included over 100 medical offices, 27 churches, 28 apartment complexes, 10 children's daycare facilities, 3 nursing homes, 11 school buildings, and a major medical center. Approximately 18,000 vehicles were destroyed. Thousands of jobs were lost. This storm would account for approximately 1,300 treated injuries and 161 deaths.

On that day in May, these peaceful communities in the southwest corner of Missouri would serve as a backdrop—the state of Missouri, the entire United States, and many nations around the world watching as the worst day in Joplin history unfolded. The whole world saw.

There were many heroes who emerged that day, often overlooked in the large picture. Joplin and Duquesne officials stepped up to the plate to meet the immense challenges. The police and fire departments, ambulance departments with the EMTs and paramedics, area sheriff's offices, Missouri Highway Patrol, and the National Guard all did what they could with limited resources under extreme conditions. The medical community, with doctors and nurses from two major hospitals and numerous medical offices, were able to treat the multitude of critical injuries under the worst possible conditions. The businesses, homes, and individuals from across the city and region that did not suffer catastrophic damage opened their hearts to reach out and assist those affected families. The whole world saw.

The churches put down their banners that said, "I am a Baptist," or "I am a Presbyterian," or "I am a Lutheran, or a Catholic, or a Pentecostal, or Methodist, etc."—banners that had been used to separate and distinguish the various denominations from each other. As the banners were laid down, people's arms went out to embrace, and comfort, and provide for those who were hardest hit—no questions asked. The churches started to do what they were supposed to do all along: "Love your neighbor." From my viewpoint, now nearly 9 months later, it seems that the churches have not picked those banners back up. The people of this community seem considerably different. And the whole world is still watching.

There are words used to describe the storm and its effects. The terms "damage," "debris," "destruction," and "death" are common. There are many "unpleasant" things that were associated with that single day. The descriptions are not all negative. Many people hang on to terms such as "hope," "faith," "mercy," "grace," and "love." There are also visual images that we use to relate to our perception of the storm. Some people associate the many crosses that popped up amid the destruction as signs of the mercy and grace of God that helped them to make it through the storm. Others think of a huge, dark, billowy cloud, with a crisp silver lining from the sun hidden behind it, as a sign of hope beyond the darkness. When you hear the testimonies of the people who faced the storm, you start to see that there were also some "very good" things.

One visual image that I have of the storm is a head of lettuce. Think of a head of lettuce that has been slightly ignored or overlooked. The leaves on the outside become brown and wilted. They are just ugly. The first inclination is to just pitch the whole thing; to basically give up on it. But when you peel that first layer of ugly shell off, you see that things aren't nearly as bad. You peel off another layer that is not quite as ugly as the first and get to another layer that is much better. By the time you get through the "ugly yuck" covering, you discover that the leaves near the heart inside are fresh and crisp, with no resemblance to the outside covering.

This storm had plenty of the ugly outside to go around. There were many layers to that "ugly" covering. This book is not intended to take away or minimize the loss and suffering that is associated with the storm. Those ugly leaves on the outside of that head of lettuce were not imaginary. The hope that I have for this book is to show that, when you eventually get below the surface to the heart, you will realize that there was a lot more to the storm than just that ugly outside covering.

(Angel carving from a storm-damaged tree trunk—Joplin tornado, 2011.
Carved by Tim Eastlake.)

CHAPTER 1
PURPOSE

M any of my patients, friends, and family often comment about my irregular sleep habits. For many years, I have gotten used to short intervals of sleep throughout any given night. If I went to bed at midnight, I may be wide awake by 3 a.m. I might be up for a few hours then take another "nap" from 5 a.m. to 7 a.m., then get up and go to work. Sometimes I read or do some laundry. I might go to the grocery store or watch television; usually nothing of much intrinsic value during those hours. Sometimes I go out on the back porch swing and use the quiet time to pray.

On Saturday morning, July 16, 2011, I was resting on the porch swing at about 4:30 a.m., taking advantage of an opportunity for quiet prayer. In my mind's eye, I could see myself holding a book. There were several details that caught my attention. I could see the color of the cover and an approximate size of the hard-bound book. I saw the size and details of the photo in the center of the cover. I remember the color of the title letters, the script, the font, and the name of the book. When I looked at the lower binding of the book, I noticed that the cover was colored and there was no jacket. I could get an idea of how thick the book was. The name on the front of the book was "*... And The Angels Came.*"

The first thought that came to my mind immediately in prayer was, "Lord, this looks like a lot of work." The feeling I received immediately was that "He would help."

I thought about this project for a day or two before I

told my wife, Rosie. She was immediately supportive. I have used her insights and opinions to help me get through some of the more complicated interviews. Rosie would help arrange the interviews so both of us could sit down with the person or families. We would record their testimonies to transcribe, compile, and share. It has been very uplifting to be able to hear these stories firsthand from the people who have witnessed or experienced these unique events.

We have heard some amazing stories. There were many circulating out there. In the days immediately after the storm, those stories would help provide some comfort to those families who suffered the wrath of the storm. Some stories might describe something that depicted the sheer power of the natural storm. Other stories might describe miraculous occurrences of survival where death seemed cheated. Are those stories encouraging, uplifting, and interesting? Most likely. Are they accurate and true? Maybe. Are they verifiable? No. For our credibility and accountability, those stories that could not be verified as firsthand accounts were not included here.

Over the next several months, we had numerous patients and friends tell us of yet another lead or two for a potential story that we might track down. Some leads were good. Many were very tortuous to follow. Some leads were just too vague to track very far. There were some stories, though credible, that did not fit into the outline for this book.

One point that I hope is evident from the stories included in this book is that there was a lot more to this storm than pain, suffering, destruction, and death. There was pain in this storm. There was suffering in this storm. There was destruction in this storm. And there was death in this storm. This is not an attempt to reduce the importance or presence of those characteristics in any way. The purpose of this book is to remind us that there were also numerous miraculous occurrences and events that took place that day that defy mere chance. I don't profess to know the answers to the "why" questions that went through people's minds after the storm, but I do believe God had His Hand on the people of Joplin in a big way. My hope here is that this compilation of stories will help others see that as well.

Several times after receiving God's vision for this book, I questioned in prayer what I needed to do. I was frequently asking for direction, guidance, and support. The response that always came was that everybody I needed to talk to, and every person I needed to work with to complete this project, would be supplied.

There was one story that we were pursuing. It was truly a unique story. We had tried unsuccessfully to meet with the individual and missed at least three opportunities for an interview with them. Rosie and I both felt that this individual had a truly amazing story and looked forward to getting the elusive interview. I only had the person's cell number. Their home phone was unlisted and we really did not have a good way to contact this individual. Finally, one Sunday evening, I asked in prayer that, "If this person's testimony was to be included in this book, there would have to be a provision that God made for me to get more information." When I got to work Monday morning, I had received an e-mail from a family member of this individual suggesting that I contact them. I now had that contact number, and the door was opened. The interview took place, and the story was included. Prayers do get answered.

I hope you enjoy reading these stories and I pray that you will be uplifted and encouraged by the testimony of the people who experienced the events that unfolded that day.

CHAPTER 2
ANGELS IN SCRIPTURE

I n this chapter, we will explore what the Bible tells us about angels. Though not all-inclusive, this section lays the groundwork and basis of what is known about angels.

What is an angel? The word "angel" comes from the Greek word *aggelos*, pronounced *angelos*, which means "**messenger**." The matching Hebrew word *mal'ak* has the same meaning, but it usually describes the whole range of spirits whom God created, including special categories such as cherubim, seraphim, and the archangels.

For those people who believe in the record of Scripture, you can completely trust in the Bible's teaching and references on angels. The Bible is your guarantee that angels do in fact exist.

Angels are mentioned inclusively in at least 34 books of the Bible, more than 115 times in the Old Testament, and 170 times in the New Testament. They are referenced from the very earliest books, whether Genesis or Job, through the last book of Revelation. There is ample information available to allow us to build a foundation for our knowledge of angelic beings.

Every reference to an angel found there is incidental to another topic. They are not the center of the attention or treated as the point of the matter in themselves. Their mention is always intended to inform us further about God, what He is doing, and how He is doing it. The details about the angels themselves are not pertinent to that purpose.

There is much fascination with angels today, in print as well as television. Although presented for entertainment purposes, those representations may illustrate a very poor grasp of what the Bible teaches about angels and God, or even definite distortions of Scripture.

Although you may or may not see angels with your physical eyes, they exist in great multitudes. While many of the exact details concerning angels are not presented in the Bible, it is still important to remember that angels, like everything else in the universe, are created by God, the Father...

"Blessed be your glorious name, exalted above all blessing and praise! You're the one, God, You alone; You made the heavens, the heavens of heavens, and all angels; The earth and everything on it, the seas and everything in them; You keep them all alive; heaven's angels worship you!"—**Nehemiah 9:6 (MSG)**

"IN THE beginning [before all time] was the Word (Christ), and the Word was with God, and the Word was God Himself.

"He was present originally with God.

"All things were made and came into existence through Him; and without Him was not even one thing made that has come into being."—**John 1:1-3 (AMP)**

Scripture speaks about the creation of angels; therefore, it is clear that they have not existed from all eternity. When they were created is not clearly specified, but they were present when the foundations of the earth were laid. Angels, like man, were directly created by a special act of God sometime prior to the existence of man. They did not evolve into being. They were often referred to as "sons of God," which would indicate that they were a direct creation of God, as Adam is also referred to as "the son of God." We are called "sons of men," but angels are never called "sons of angels." Angels are not a race

6

descended from a common ancestor. They are supernatural beings, distinctly separate from the race of man.

Contrary to various popular depictions in print and film, people do not become angels upon their death. Angels are not glorified human beings. Angels and humans are two separate groups...

"You are the only Lord. You made the heavens, even the highest heavens, with all the stars. You made the earth and everything on it, the seas and everything in them; you give life to everything. The heavenly army worships you."—**Nehemiah 9:6 (NCV)**

"Let them praise the name of the LORD, For He commanded and they were created."—**Psalm 148:5 (NKJV)**

"Where were you when I laid the earth's foundation? Tell me, if you understand. Who marked off its dimensions? Surely you know! Who stretched a measuring line across it? On what were its footings set, or who laid its cornerstone—while the morning stars sang together and all the angels shouted for joy?"—**Job 38:4-7 (NIV)**

"But you have come to Mount Zion and to the city of the living God, the heavenly Jerusalem, and to myriads of angels, to the general assembly and church of the firstborn who are enrolled in heaven, and to God, the Judge of all, and to the spirits of the righteous made perfect..."—**Hebrews 12:22-23 (NASB)**

Angels are spiritual beings created by God to glorify, worship, praise, and serve Him...

"For by Him all things were created that are in heaven and that are on earth, visible and invisible, whether thrones or dominions or principalities or powers. All things were created through Him and for Him."—**Colossians 1:16 (NKJV)**

"You alone are the Lord. You made heaven, the highest heaven, with all its armies. You made the earth and everything on it, the seas and everything in them. You give life to them all, and

the armies of heaven worship you."—**Nehemiah 9:6 (GW)**

"But when He again brings the firstborn into the world, He says: 'Let all the angels of God worship Him.'"—**Hebrews 1:6 (NKJV)**

"All the angels stood around the throne with the leaders and the four living creatures. They bowed in front of the throne with their faces touching the ground, worshiped God…"—**Revelation 7:11 (GW)**

"Praise Him, all you angels. Praise Him, all you armies of heaven. Praise Him, sun and moon. Praise Him, all you shining stars. Praise Him, highest heavens and you waters above the sky. Let them praise the Lord, because they were created by His command."—**Psalm 148:2-5 (NCV)**

"Suddenly, a large army of angels appeared with the angel. They were praising God by saying…"—**Luke 2:13 (GW)**

"Then I looked and heard the voice of many angels, numbering thousands upon thousands, and ten thousand times ten thousand. They encircled the throne and the living creatures and the elders. In a loud voice they were saying:

"'Worthy is the Lamb, who was slain, to receive power and wealth and wisdom and strength and honor and glory and praise!'"—**Revelation 5:11-12 (NIV)**

As created beings, angels are mere creatures. The angels are inferior to God. They are not deity. They are not God and should not be revered or worshiped as God and do not accept sacrifices. The Bible is very clear that they cannot be in different places at the same time. They must have some localized presence. They are not omnipresent. They cannot be everywhere at once. They must go somewhere to get somewhere. They are neither omnipotent (all-powerful) nor omniscient (all-knowing.) Angels have greater power and wisdom than man, but both are limited. As a separate order of creatures, they have powers and abilities far beyond ours in this present age, but as separate creatures, they too are limited in their powers, knowledge, and activities under God's authority and judgment…

"Manoah said to the Messenger of the Lord, 'Please stay while we prepare a young goat for you to eat.'

"But the Messenger of the Lord responded, 'If I stay here, I will not eat any of your food. But if you make a burnt offering, sacrifice it to the Lord.' (Manoah did not realize that it was the Messenger of the Lord.)"—**Judges 13:15-16 (GW)**

"And I fell at his feet to worship him. But he said to me, 'See that you do not do that! I am your fellow servant, and of your brethren who have the testimony of Jesus. Worship God! For the testimony of Jesus is the spirit of prophecy.'"—**Revelation 19:10 (NKJV)**

"Then he continued, 'Do not be afraid, Daniel. Since the first day that you set your mind to gain understanding and to humble yourself before your God, your words were heard, and I have come in response to them. But the prince of the Persian kingdom resisted me twenty-one days. Then Michael, one of the chief princes, came to help me, because I was detained there with the king of Persia.'"—**Daniel 10:12-13 (NIV)**

"But of that [exact] day and hour no one knows, not even the angels of heaven, nor the Son, but only the Father."—**Matthew 24:36 (AMPC)**

"But even the angels, who are much stronger and more powerful than false teachers, do not accuse them with insults before the Lord."—**2 Peter 2:11 (NCV)**

Angels are holy…

"When the Son of Man comes in His glory (His majesty and splendor), and all the holy angels with Him, then He will sit on the throne of His glory."—**Matthew 25:31 (AMPC)**

Angels are innumerable. There are as many angels as

there are stars in the heavens. Based on the biblically inspired calculations of Hilton Sutton (an authority on biblical prophecy,) there are 100 trillion angels available to the Body of Christ to carry out God's will on the earth. With an estimated world population of approximately 8 billion people as of 2023, that would allocate about 12,500 angels per person on the planet...

"But you have come to Mount Zion and to the city of the living God, the heavenly Jerusalem, to an innumerable company of angels..."—**Hebrews 12:22 (NKJV)**
"A fiery stream issued and came forth from before Him. A thousand thousands ministered to Him; ten thousand times ten thousand stood before Him. The court was seated, and the books were opened."—**Daniel 7:10 (NKJV)**

"The chariots of God are twenty thousand, even thousands of thousands; the Lord is among them as in Sinai, in the Holy Place."—**Psalm 68:17 (NKJV)**

"Then I looked, and I heard the voices of many angels on every side of the throne and of the living creatures and the elders [of the heavenly Sanhedrin], and they numbered ten thousand times ten thousand and thousands of thousands..."—**Revelation 5:11 (AMPC)**

"Do you suppose that I cannot appeal to My Father, and He will immediately provide Me with more than twelve legions [more than 80,000] of angels?"—**Matthew 26:53 (AMPC)**

The number of angels, completed at their creation, is forever fixed. Unlike humans or animals who are created in pairs and procreate, angels were created simultaneously as a host or company, a countless host of myriads. They do not marry or reproduce. New angels are not being added. As they are not subject to death or any form of extinction, they do not decrease in number...

"...and they can no longer die; for they are like the angels..."—**Luke 20:36 (NIV)**

Throughout the Bible, the various angels are referred to by different names. They are referred to as ministers, with religious duties and spiritual service. They are called hosts, depicting their military service. The name chariots may refer to their swiftness. They are watchers, as supervisors and agents. They are named sons of the Mighty, sons of God, holy ones, saints, and stars...

"Bless the LORD, you His angels, who excel in strength, who do His word, heeding the voice of His word. Bless the LORD, all you His hosts, you ministers of His, who do His pleasure."—**Psalm 103:20-21 (NKJV)**

"Who makes His angels spirits, His ministers a flame of fire."—**Psalm 104:4 (NKJV)**

"And He said, No [neither], but as Prince of the Lord's host have I now come. And Joshua fell on his face to the earth and worshiped, and said to Him, What says my Lord to His servant?"—**Joshua 5:14 (AMPC)**

"[Elisha] answered, Fear not; for those with us are more than those with them.

"Then Elisha prayed, Lord, I pray You, open his eyes that he may see. And the Lord opened the young man's eyes, and he saw, and behold, the mountain was full of horses and chariots of fire round about Elisha."—**2 Kings 6:16-17 (AMPC)**

"The chariots of God are twenty thousand, even thousands upon thousands. The Lord is among them as He was in Sinai, [so also] in the Holy Place (the sanctuary in Jerusalem)."—**Psalm 68:17 (AMPC)**

"I saw in the visions of my head [as I lay] on my bed, and behold, a watcher, a holy one, came down

from heaven."—**Daniel 4:13 (AMPC)**

"The guardians have announced this decision. The holy ones have announced this so that every living creature will know that the Most High has power over human kingdoms. He gives them to whomever he wishes. He can place the lowest of people in charge of them.'"—**Daniel 4:17 (GW)**

"Then I heard a holy one speaking, and another holy one said to him, 'How long will it take for the vision to be fulfilled—the vision concerning the daily sacrifice, the rebellion that causes desolation, the surrender of the sanctuary and the trampling underfoot of the LORD's people?'"—**Daniel 8:13 (NIV)**

"Praise Him, all His angels; Praise Him, all His hosts! Praise Him, sun and moon; Praise Him, all you stars of light!"—**Psalm 148:2-3 (NKJV)**

God has assigned multitudes of angels to carry out the terms of His covenant with us. **Angels worship the Person of God. They watch and observe God's people. They rejoice in God's creation and His redemption, and they constantly serve Him and perform the will of God. On earth they inform, instruct, and interpret God's will and word. In the Bible, there are records that the angels have ministered to Daniel, Zechariah, Zacharias, Mary and Joseph, the shepherds, the women at the tomb, the apostles, Philip, Cornelius, and John.** They are ministering spirits sent out to minister and render service for the sake of those who will inherit salvation. Though God can always act independently, without the use of agents, He has chosen to use both angelic and human instruments to accomplish His will. Throughout the Bible, angels can be found acting as God's servants in various ministry tasks.

While there is not a specific passage that states the existence of a guardian angel, Scripture does speak of those angels appointed by God with specific duties to watch over the elect, to guard and protect as a guardian angel. There are also references to suggest a guardian over the little children. The early churches understood that each Believer had a special angel to minister to their physical needs...

"And they do not rest day or night, saying: 'Holy, holy, holy, Lord God Almighty, who was and is and is to come!'"—**Revelation 4:8 (NKJV)**

"Now Jesus has gone into heaven and is at God's right side ruling over angels, authorities, and powers."—**1 Peter 3:22 (NCV)**

"Beware that you do not despise or feel scornful toward or think little of one of these little ones, for I tell you that in heaven their angels always are in the presence of and look upon the face of My Father Who is in heaven."—**Matthew 18:10 (AMPC)**

"Likewise, I say to you, there is joy in the presence of the angels of God over one sinner who repents."—**Luke 15:10 (NKJV)**

"Give unto the LORD, O you mighty ones, give unto the LORD glory and strength. Give unto the LORD the glory due to His name; worship the LORD in the beauty of holiness."—**Psalm 29:1-2 (NKJV)**

"You who are His angels, praise the Lord. You are the mighty warriors who do what He says and who obey His voice. You, His armies, praise the Lord; you are His servants who do what He wants."—**Psalm 103:20-21 (NCV)**

"[The purpose is] that through the church the complicated, many-sided wisdom of God in all its infinite variety and innumerable aspects might now be made known to the angelic rulers and authorities (principalities and powers) in the heavenly sphere."—**Ephesians 3:10 (AMPC)**

"Are not the angels all ministering spirits (servants) sent out in the service [of God for the assistance] of those who are to inherit salvation?"—**Hebrews 1:14 (AMPC)**

*"Who makes His angels spirits, His ministers a
flame of fire."*—**Psalm 104:4 (NKJV)**

*"Why, then, was the law given at all? It was added
because of transgressions until the Seed to whom the promise
referred had come. The law was given through angels and
entrusted to a mediator."*—**Galatians 3:19 (NIV)**

*"For He will command His angels concerning you to guard you in
all your ways; they will lift you up in their hands, so that you will
not strike your foot against a stone."*—**Psalm 91:11-12 (NIV)**

*"The LORD God of heaven, who took me from my father's
house and from the land of my family, and who spoke to me
and swore to me, saying, 'To your descendants I give this
land,' He will send His angel before you, and you shall take
a wife for my son from there."*—**Genesis 24:7 (NKJV)**

Angels provide both protection from danger and
deliverance from danger. They can impart physical strength to
man in his time of need. They have supplied man with food for
nourishment...

*"For He will give His angels [especial] charge over you to
accompany and defend and preserve you in all your ways
[of obedience and service]."*—**Psalm 91:11 (AMPC)**

*"But the men [the angels] reached out and pulled Lot into
the house to them and shut the door after him.*

*"And they struck the men who were at the door of the house
with blindness [which dazzled them], from the youths to
the old men, so that they wearied themselves [groping]
to find the door."*—**Genesis 19:10-11 (AMPC)**

*"And when the servant of the man of God arose early and went out,
there was an army, surrounding the city with horses and chariots.
And his servant said to him, 'Alas, my master! What shall we do?'*

"So he answered, 'Do not fear, for those who are with us are more than those who are with them.' And Elisha prayed, and said, 'Lord, I pray, open his eyes that he may see.' Then the Lord opened the eyes of the young man, and he saw. And behold, the mountain was full of horses and chariots of fire all around Elisha."—**2 Kings 6:15-18 (NKJV)**

"The two angels came to Sodom in the evening as Lot was sitting near the city gate. When he saw them, he got up and went to them and bowed facedown on the ground... At dawn the next morning, the angels begged Lot to hurry. They said, 'Go! Take your wife and your two daughters with you so you will not be destroyed when the city is punished.'"—**Genesis 19:1, 15 (NCV)**

"My God sent His angel and shut the lions' mouths so that they couldn't hurt me. He did this because He considered me innocent. Your Majesty, I haven't committed any crime."—**Daniel 6:22 (GW)**

"Do you suppose that I cannot appeal to My Father, and He will immediately provide Me with more than twelve legions [more than 80,000] of angels?"—**Matthew 26:53 (AMPC)**

"...by arresting the apostles and putting them in the city jail. But at night an angel from the Lord opened the doors to their cell and led them out of the prison."—**Acts 5:18-19 (GW)**

"The angel of the LORD encamps around those who fear Him, and rescues them."—**Psalm 34:7 (NASB)**

"'How can I talk to you, sir? I have no strength left, and the wind has been knocked out of me.' Again, the person who looked like a human touched me, and I became stronger. He said, 'Don't be afraid. You are highly respected. Everything is alright! Be strong! Be strong!' As he talked to me, I became stronger. I said, 'Sir, tell me what you came to say. You have strengthened me.'"—**Daniel 10:17-19 (GW)**

"So the devil left Jesus, and angels came and took care of Him."—**Matthew 4:11 (NCV)**

"And He stayed in the wilderness (desert) forty days, being tempted [all the while] by Satan; and He was with the wild beasts, and the angels ministered to Him [continually]."—**Mark 1:13 (AMPC)**

"Then an angel from heaven appeared to Him to strengthen Him"—**Luke 22:43 (NCV)**

"Then as he lay and slept under a broom tree, suddenly an angel touched him, and said to him, 'Arise and eat.'"—**1 Kings 19:5 (NKJV)**

"He taught me and said to me, 'Daniel, I have come to give you wisdom and to help you understand. When you first started praying, an answer was given, and I came to tell you, because God loves you very much. So think about the message and understand the vision.'"—**Daniel 9:22-23 (NCV)**

"Now I have come to make you understand what is to befall your people in the latter days, for the vision is for [many] days yet to come."—**Daniel 10:14 (AMPC)**

The angels also serve as a supernatural means of communication between God and man. They provide encouragement, comfort, and answer to prayer. God sent angels to provide sustenance for Jesus at the end of His 40 days in the wilderness. He has undoubtedly done the same for people today. Angels also give man guidance, direction, and revelation...

"And the angel replied to him, I am Gabriel. I stand in the [very] presence of God, and I have been sent to talk to you and to bring you this good news."—**Luke 1:19 (AMPC)**

"Last night an angel of the God to whom I belong and whom I serve stood beside me and said, 'Do not be afraid, Paul. You must stand trial before Caesar; and God has graciously given you the lives of all who sail with you.'"—**Acts 27:23-24 (NIV)**

"Then a hand touched me and made my hands and knees shake.

The man said to me, 'Daniel, you are highly respected. Pay attention to my words. Stand up, because I've been sent to you.' When he said this to me, I stood up, trembling. He told me, 'Don't be afraid, Daniel. God has heard everything that you said ever since the first day you decided to humble yourself in front of your God so that you could learn to understand things. I have come in response to your prayer.'"—**Daniel 10:10-12 (GW)**

"While I was saying these things in my prayer to the Lord, my God, confessing my sins and the sins of the people of Israel and praying for God's holy hill, Gabriel came to me. (I had seen him in my last vision.) He came flying quickly to me about the time of the evening sacrifice, while I was still praying. He taught me and said to me, 'Daniel, I have come to give you wisdom and to help you understand. When you first started praying, an answer was given, and I came to tell you, because God loves you very much. So think about the message and understand the vision.'"—**Daniel 9:20-23 (NCV)**

"Suddenly an angel of the Lord appeared and a light shone in the cell. He struck Peter on the side and woke him up. 'Quick, get up!' he said, and the chains fell off Peter's wrists. Then the angel said to him, 'Put on your clothes and sandals.' And Peter did so. 'Wrap your cloak around you and follow me,' the angel told him. Peter followed him out of the prison, but he had no idea that what the angel was doing was really happening; he thought he was seeing a vision. They passed the first and second guards and came to the iron gate leading to the city. It opened for them by itself, and they went through it. When they had walked the length of one street, suddenly the angel left him."—**Acts 12:7-10 (NIV)**

"Then as he lay and slept under a broom tree, suddenly an angel touched him, and said to him, 'Arise and eat.'"—**1 Kings 19:5 (NKJV)**

"Now in the sixth month [after that], the angel Gabriel was sent from God to a town of Galilee named Nazareth,..."—**Luke 1:26 (AMPC)**

"But after he had considered this, an angel of the Lord appeared to him in a dream and said, 'Joseph son of David, do not be afraid to take Mary home as your wife, because what is conceived in her is from the Holy Spirit.'"—**Matthew 1:20 (NIV)**

"Now when they had departed, behold, an angel of the Lord appeared to Joseph in a dream, saying, 'Arise, take the young Child and His mother, flee to Egypt, and stay there until I bring you word; for Herod will seek the young Child to destroy Him.'"—**Matthew 2:13 (NKJV)**

"Now an angel of the Lord said to Philip, 'Go south to the road—the desert road—that goes down from Jerusalem to Gaza.'"—**Acts 8:26 (NIV)**

"One day at about three in the afternoon he had a vision. He distinctly saw an angel of God, who came to him and said, 'Cornelius!'

"Cornelius stared at him in fear. 'What is it, Lord?' he asked.

"The angel answered, 'Your prayers and gifts to the poor have come up as a memorial offering before God. Now send men to Joppa to bring back a man named Simon who is called Peter. He is staying with Simon the tanner, whose house is by the sea.'"—**Acts 10:3-6 (NIV)**

"The angel said to me, 'These words can be trusted and are true.' The Lord, the God of the spirits of the prophets, sent his angel to show his servants the things that must happen soon."—**Revelation 22:6 (NCV)**

"He had a dream in which he saw a stairway resting on the earth, with its top reaching to heaven, and the angels of God were ascending and descending on it."—**Genesis 28:12 (NIV)**

Angels deliver and minister to the Believer even at the moment of death. One angel went with Moses to deliver two and a half million people through the wilderness for 40 years.

One angel protected three men from even being singed or smoke covered while inside a super-hot furnace. One angel sealed the mouths of lions to protect Daniel while he was in the lion's den. A single angel slew 185,000 people in one night...

"All the angels are spirits who serve God and are sent to help those who will receive salvation."—**Hebrews 1:14 (NCV)**

"For He will give His angels [especial] charge over you to accompany and defend and preserve you in all your ways [of obedience and service]."—**Psalm 91:11 (AMPC)**

"But during the night an angel of the Lord opened the doors of the jail and brought them out."—**Acts 5:19 (NIV)**

"So the devil left Jesus, and angels came and took care of Him."—**Matthew 4:11 (NCV)**

"You make your angels winds and your servants flames of fire."—**Psalm 104:4 (GW)**

"This is what God said about the angels: 'God makes his angels become like winds. He makes his servants become like flames of fire.'"—**Hebrews 1:7 (NCV)**

"The time came when the beggar died and the angels carried him to Abraham's side. The rich man also died and was buried."—**Luke 16:22 (NIV)**

"Behold, I am going to send an angel before you to guard you along the way and to bring you into the place which I have prepared. Be attentive to him and obey his voice; do not be rebellious toward him, for he will not pardon your rebellion, since My name is in him. But if you truly obey his voice and do all that I say, then I will be an enemy to your enemies and an adversary to your adversaries. For My angel will go before you and bring you into the land of the Amorites, the Hittites, the Perizzites, the Canaanites, the Hivites, and the Jebusites; and I will completely destroy them."—**Exodus 23:20-23 (NASB)**

"Then Nebuchadnezzar said, Blessed be the God of Shadrach, Meshach, and Abednego, Who has sent His angel and delivered His servants who believed in, trusted in, and relied on Him! And they set aside the king's command and yielded their bodies rather than serve or worship any god except their own God."— **Daniel 3:28 (AMP)**

"My God sent His angel and shut the lions' mouths, so that they have not hurt me, because I was found innocent before Him; and also, O king, I have done no wrong before you."—**Daniel 6:22 (NKJV)**

"And it all came to pass, for that night the Angel of the Lord went forth and slew 185,000 in the camp of the Assyrians; and when [the living] arose early in the morning, behold, all these were dead bodies."—**2 Kings 19:35 (AMPC)**

Angels are spirit beings. However, on two specific occasions, they are described as partaking physical food and once applying physical force...

"He then brought some curds and milk and the calf that had been prepared, and set these before them. While they ate, he stood near them under a tree."—**Genesis 18:8 (NIV)**

"But he insisted so strongly that they did go with him and entered his house. He prepared a meal for them, baking bread without yeast, and they ate."—**Genesis 19:3 (NIV)**

"Suddenly an angel of the Lord appeared and a light shone in the cell. He struck Peter on the side and woke him up. 'Quick, get up!' he said, and the chains fell off Peter's wrists."—**Acts 12:7 (NIV)**

Angels are extremely strong with superhuman strength and exceptionally smart. They are swifter than men. They are not bound by laws of time, nature, and gravity. They are not hindered by man's fallen nature...

"Bless the LORD, you His angels, who excel in strength, who do His word, heeding the voice of His word. Bless the LORD, all you His hosts, you ministers of His, who

do His pleasure."—**Psalm 103:20-21 (NKJV)**

"...and give relief to you who are troubled, and to us as well. This will happen when the Lord Jesus is revealed from heaven in blazing fire with his powerful angels."—**2 Thessalonians 1:7 (NIV)**

"And it all came to pass, for that night the Angel of the Lord went forth and slew 185,000 in the camp of the Assyrians; and when [the living] arose early in the morning, behold, all these were dead bodies."—**2 Kings 19:35 (AMPC)**

"Whereas [even] angels, though superior in might and power, do not bring a defaming charge against them before the Lord."—**2 Peter 2:11 (AMPC)**

"Then I saw another angel flying in midair, and he had the eternal gospel to proclaim to those who live on the earth—to every nation, tribe, language and people."—**Revelation 14:6 (NIV)**

"Do you suppose that I cannot appeal to My Father, and He will immediately provide Me with more than twelve legions [more than 80,000] of angels?"—**Matthew 26:53 (AMPC)**

Angels can speak and give direction...

"Now an angel of the Lord said to Philip, 'Go south to the road—the desert road—that goes down from Jerusalem to Gaza.'"—**Acts 8:26 (NIV)**

Angels possess separate and individual personalities— no two are alike. They are extremely intelligent, but not all-knowing. They possess will and emotion, joy, and desire...

"Joab did it so you would see things differently. My master, you are wise like an angel of God who knows everything that happens on earth."—**2 Samuel 14:20 (NCV)**

"But of that [exact] day and hour no one knows, not even the angels of heaven, nor the Son, but only the Father."—**Matthew 24:36 (AMPC)**

"…while I was still in prayer, Gabriel, the man I had seen in the earlier vision, came to me in swift flight about the time of the evening sacrifice. He instructed me and said to me, 'Daniel, I have now come to give you insight and understanding.'"—**Daniel 9:21-22 (NIV)**

"…while the morning stars sang together and all the angels shouted for joy?"—**Job 38:7 (NIV)**

"It was revealed to them that they were not serving themselves but you, when they spoke of the things that have now been told you by those who have preached the gospel to you by the Holy Spirit sent from heaven. Even angels long to look into these things."—**1 Peter 1:12 (NIV)**

Angels work closely with or have some control over different creatures of the animal kingdom in carrying out their ministry…

"And Elisha prayed, 'Open his eyes, LORD, so that he may see.' Then the LORD opened the servant's eyes, and he looked and saw the hills full of horses and chariots of fire all around Elisha."—**2 Kings 6:17 (NIV)**

"And the armies in heaven, clothed in fine linen, white and clean, followed Him on white horses."— **Revelation 19:14 (NKJV)**

Angels are generally invisible beings. On occasion, they have manifested themselves. Angels are not men, although they may take on human form…

"While they were puzzled about this, two men in clothes that were as bright as lightning suddenly stood beside them."—**Luke 24:4 (GW)**

"They were looking intently up into the sky as he was going, when suddenly two men dressed in white stood beside them."—**Acts 1:10 (NIV)**

"Cornelius answered, 'Four days ago I was praying at home. It was

at this same time, three o'clock in the afternoon. Suddenly, a man dressed in radiant clothes stood in front of me.'"—**Acts 10:30 (GW)**

"There was a violent earthquake, for an angel of the Lord came down from heaven and, going to the tomb, rolled back the stone and sat on it. His appearance was like lightning, and his clothes were white as snow."—**Matthew 28:2-3 (NIV)**

Angels are often depicted as cute, little, "stubby-winged cupids" associated with Valentine's Day, but they are much more than "cute." There are different ranks of angels throughout the Bible. There are the named archangels. Michael, a warring angel whose name means "who is like God?" and Gabriel, the proclamation angel. There are unnamed messengers, or proclamation angels. There are cherubim and seraphim, and other "living creatures" who have similarities to both. There are "ruling angels" and there are "guardian angels…"

"Then he continued, 'Do not be afraid, Daniel. Since the first day that you set your mind to gain understanding and to humble yourself before your God, your words were heard, and I have come in response to them. But the prince of the Persian kingdom resisted me twenty-one days. Then Michael, one of the chief princes, came to help me, because I was detained there with the king of Persia.'"—**Daniel 10:12-13 (NIV)**

"And behold, there was a great earthquake, for an angel of the Lord descended from heaven and came and rolled the boulder back and sat upon it."—**Matthew 28:2 (AMPC)**

"For the Lord himself will come down from heaven, with a loud command, with the voice of the archangel and with the trumpet call of God, and the dead in Christ will rise first."—**1 Thessalonians 4:16 (NIV)**

"Then an angel appeared to Him from heaven, strengthening Him."—**Luke 22:43 (NKJV)**

"And now I urge you to take heart, for there will be no loss of life among you, but only of the ship. For there stood by me this night an angel of the God to whom I belong and whom I serve..."—**Acts 27:22-23 (NKJV)**

"Beware that you do not despise or feel scornful toward or think little of one of these little ones, for I tell you that in heaven their angels always are in the presence of and look upon the face of My Father Who is in heaven."—**Matthew 18:10 (AMPC)**

There are various notions that we all get from art and literature of what an angel should look like. When portrayed in art, they might resemble cherubs. The "guardian angel" in our artwork might show an older female angel guiding children along a path. Some pictures show even larger angels watching over sleeping children.

Biblical angels never were depicted as cute, chubby infants, they are always described as adults. When the people in the Bible saw an angel, their typical reaction was to fall to their knees in awe and fear.

One thing nearly every artistic depiction utilizes is the presence of wings. Remove the wings and all you see is a person in a robe. Many descriptions in Scripture mention nothing of wings, but there was something about them that was definitely different. The cherubim and seraphim —included in the class of angels—are described as having wings, and some others are assumed to have wings. However, many angels described definitely do not have wings in their descriptions.

In modern times, we have come to associate our perception of angels with feelings of peace, comfort, protection, guidance, etc. In biblical times, there was less of a pre-conceived notion of what angels were to look like. They were just there, and they really stood out in a crowd, or not.

There are instances where the person who saw the angel was greatly terrified by its presence or appearance. There are times when the person talking to the angel thought that they were speaking to a person. When seen in their glory, there was a special brightness upon them...

"Abraham looked up and saw three men standing nearby..."—**Genesis 18:2 (NIV)**

"Above him were seraphim, each with six wings: With two wings they covered their faces, with two they covered their feet, and with two they were flying."—**Isaiah 6:2 (NIV)**

"Yes, while I was speaking in prayer, the man Gabriel, whom I had seen in the former vision, being caused to fly swiftly, came near to me and touched me about the time of the evening sacrifice."—**Daniel 9:21 (AMPC)**

We know that angels are not men, although they can take on the appearance of an ordinary human being when the occasion demands; at times, their appearance is characterized as dazzling white and blazing glory.

When angels do appear, they generally appear in the form of men. Abraham welcomed three angelic guests who appeared at first to be nothing more than some travelers in Genesis 18. In the next chapter, the two angels who went to Sodom were described simply as a pair of human visitors. In at least one instance, an angel is described as female in appearance, rather than male. In some instances, they are described as men with unusual features...

"Do not forget to show hospitality to strangers, for by so doing some people have shown hospitality to angels without knowing it."—**Hebrews 13:2 (NIV)**

"And Elisha prayed, 'Open his eyes, LORD, so that he may see.' Then the LORD opened the servant's eyes, and he looked and saw the hills full of horses and chariots

of fire all around Elisha."—**2 Kings 6:17 (NIV)**

"And going into the tomb, they saw a young man sitting [there] on the right [side], clothed in a [long, stately, sweeping] robe of white, and they were utterly amazed and struck with terror."—**Mark 16:5 (AMPC)**

"And while they were perplexed and wondering what to do about this, behold, two men in dazzling raiment suddenly stood beside them."—**Luke 24:4 (AMPC)**

"…and the seven angels who had the seven plagues came out of the temple, clothed in linen, clean and bright, and their chests wrapped with golden sashes."—**Revelation 15:6 (NASB)**

"And behold, there was a great earthquake, for an angel of the Lord descended from heaven and came and rolled the boulder back and sat upon it.

"His appearance was like lightning, and his garments as white as snow.

"And those keeping guard were so frightened at the sight of him that they were agitated and they trembled and became like dead men."—**Matthew 28:2-4 (AMPC)**

"He created all things in heaven and on earth, visible and invisible. Whether they are kings or lords, rulers or powers—everything has been created through him and for him."—**Colossians 1:16 (GW)**

"Then I raised my eyes and looked, and there were two women, coming with the wind in their wings; for they had wings like the wings of a stork, and they lifted up the basket between earth and heaven."— **Zechariah 5:9 (NKJV)**

"Then I saw another mighty angel coming down from heaven, robed in a cloud, with a [halo like a] rainbow over his head; his face was like the sun, and his feet (legs) were like columns of fire."—**Revelation 10:1 (AMPC)**

"When I looked up, I saw a man dressed in linen, and he had a belt made of gold from Uphaz around his waist. His body was like beryl. His face looked like lightning. His eyes were like flaming torches. His arms and legs looked like polished bronze. When he spoke, his voice sounded like the roar of a crowd."— **Daniel 10:5-6 (GW)**

Angels have at times been fearful to look upon. Unlike references to seeing God's face with fatal results, looking upon the face of an angel will not make a person die…

"When he saw the angel, Zechariah was startled and frightened."—**Luke 1:12 (NCV)**

"And going into the tomb, they saw a young man sitting [there] on the right [side], clothed in a long, stately, sweeping] robe of white, and they were utterly amazed and struck with terror."—**Mark 16:5 (AMPC)**

"And behold, an angel of the Lord stood by them, and the glory of the Lord flashed and shone all about them, and they were terribly frightened."—**Luke 2:9 (AMPC)**

"But while he thought about these things, behold, an angel of the Lord appeared to him in a dream, saying, 'Joseph, son of David, do not be afraid to take to you Mary your wife, for that which is conceived in her is of the Holy Spirit. And she will bring forth a Son, and you shall call His name JESUS, for He will save His people from their sins.'"—**Matthew 1:20-21 (NKJV)**

"And the angel answered and said to him, 'I am Gabriel, who stands in the presence of God, and was sent to speak to you and bring you these glad tidings. But behold, you will be mute and not able to speak until the day these things take place, because you did not believe my words which will be fulfilled in their own time."—**Luke 1:19-20 (NKJV)**

"In the sixth month of Elizabeth's pregnancy, God sent the angel Gabriel to Nazareth, a town in Galilee, to a virgin pledged to

be married to a man named Joseph, a descendant of David. The virgin's name was Mary. The angel went to her and said, 'Greetings, you who are highly favored! The Lord is with you.'

"Mary was greatly troubled at his words and wondered what kind of greeting this might be. But the angel said to her, 'Do not be afraid, Mary; you have found favor with God. You will conceive and give birth to a son, and you are to call Him Jesus. He will be great and will be called the Son of the Most High. The Lord God will give Him the throne of His father David, and He will reign over Jacob's descendants forever; His kingdom will never end.'

"'How will this be,' Mary asked the angel, 'since I am a virgin?' The angel answered, 'The Holy Spirit will come on you, and the power of the Most High will overshadow you. So the holy one to be born will be called the Son of God.'"—**Luke 1:26-35 (NIV)**

"When Gideon realized that it was the angel of the LORD, he exclaimed, 'Alas, Sovereign LORD! I have seen the angel of the LORD face to face!'

"But the LORD said to him, 'Peace! Do not be afraid. You are not going to die.'"—**Judges 6:22-23 (NIV)**

Angels are messengers from God, not messengers to God. They are not teachers. There is no biblical precedent or permission to contact or commune with angels. There is no provision to love our angels or to pray to our angels. Scripture makes no mention of loving our angels or calling upon them for health, healing, prosperity, or guidance. Angels are God's servants, and all the attention, emphasis, and glory should go to God alone. Scripture is very direct in teaching us to love only God, His Word, and people. We are never instructed to pray to angels, but only to God.

There is no angel within us. They were created separately and differently, before man. When we hear a bell ring, as shown in the movie *"It's a Wonderful Life,"* it does not mean that an angel is getting its wings. Nor do good people become angels when they die. We remain human beings—not angels, and certainly not God.

The ministry of angels will never contradict the Bible. The character and actions of angels will always be consistent with the character of God. Any action, encounter, or revelation with an angel will always glorify God, and not the angel. They typically do their work and then disappear.

We are never to worship angels, as they are fellow servants with Believers, called upon to serve God. Angels are powerful and awesome, but like us, they are mere creatures and servants of God. God alone deserves our worship. We should not pray to them or put our trust in them, even though God may use them as our guardian. We are to trust God rather than angels. They minister at His bidding.

There is comfort knowing that God may protect, provide, guide, encourage, and strengthen us through supernatural means, but we are not guaranteed the certainty of that deliverance or protection. We should never presume that that provision from God will actually occur. Even considering that angels minister to people in different ways, we need to keep in mind that God does not always deliver us from danger, provide the needs that we recognize or believe in, or guide us as we wish to be led, whether by angels and miracles, or by His direct intervention. For His own sovereign purpose in His plan may include suffering or testing, a tool that allows us to grow and manifest the character of Christ.

CHAPTER 3
ANOTHER TIME, ANOTHER PLACE

T he following accounts are meant to show that supernatural occurrences, such as angelic encounters, are not limited to major catastrophic events, such as a massive tornado, or found only in a Midwestern city in the middle of the Bible belt. There are many other instances found throughout the world such as these; you may even have your own. God is always on the move…

◆ ◆ ◆

"Are not the angels all ministering spirits (servants) sent out in the service [of God for the assistance] of those who are to inherit salvation?"—**Hebrews 1:14 (AMPC)**

The following two testimonies were from different missionaries who also came forward during our interview phase. Although from a different time and place, they recognized the ministering spirits that presented in their individual situations. They both acknowledged they were witness to supernatural interventions affecting their individual environments and circumstances. Their perceptions of the occurrences are very similar to those with stories from Joplin.

The first story involves a woman who worked alone as a missionary on a compound in northern Africa. There had been riots in the area between some members of the local tribes. As the rioting warriors were advancing on the dirt roads toward the houses where the white intruders lived, she hid in the closet and prayed. As she waited huddled in that closet, she never heard any of the angry rioters. When she came out of the safety of the closet, she saw that no one had even entered her building. There was no sign of damage or unrest to her compound. The woman learned later that those angry rioters, intent on killing the white intruders and burning down their buildings, were turned away from entering the compound by tall, white-clothed warriors wielding large swords. The rioters left everything untouched.

Another missionary on a medical mission in a small field hospital in Africa reported a similar story. The missionary had to travel through jungle roads by bicycle to get supplies in a nearby city about every two weeks or so. The trip would take two days each way, which meant he would have to camp in the jungle along the way. Once, while he was in the city picking up supplies, he came across two men who were fighting. One of them had become seriously injured in the fight. The missionary treated the injured man and talked to him about Jesus; afterward, he began the first part of his return trip through the jungle, bringing him safely home the next day.

When he returned to the city two weeks later on his regular trip for supplies, he came across the man whose injuries he had treated. The treated man told him that he knew that the missionary carried money and medicine. The man told the missionary that he had talked to some of his friends in the city that first day and they followed the missionary into the jungle, knowing he would camp overnight. They had planned on waiting for him to go to sleep so they could kill him and take his money and medicine. Just as the group was getting ready to move into the campsite, they stopped because the men saw the missionary was surrounded by 26 armed guards as he slept.

The missionary dismissed the story as he was truly by himself on the trip home through the jungle that night. However, the man was insistent and told him that he and his friends all saw the 26 men around the campsite. The man and his friends were afraid and left the missionary alone.

As the missionary was telling the story to the congregation of his home church during a visit to the United States, one of the men in the church stood up and asked if the missionary could tell him the exact date of the encounter. The missionary recalled the date and then the man who had asked the question told his part of the story. Though it had been night for the missionary in Africa, it had been morning in the USA—as the man was preparing to play a round of golf that day, he felt the Lord urging him to pray for the missionary. The man felt that urge so strongly, that he called a number of men in the church to join in prayer for the missionary. In conclusion, the man asked all the men he had called to pray to stand up with him. All 26 men stood together—the exact number of angelic beings who came to guard the missionary.

◆ ◆ ◆

"Then a hand touched me and made my hands and knees shake. The man said to me, 'Daniel, you are highly respected. Pay attention to my words. Stand up, because I've been sent to you.' When he said this to me, I stood up, trembling. He told me, 'Don't be afraid, Daniel. God has heard everything that you said ever since the first day you decided to humble yourself in front of your God so that you could learn to understand things. I have come in response to your prayer.'"—**Daniel 10:10-12 (GW)**

This next story took place many years ago in an unrelated event in Georgia. John was referred to us with his testimony, shortly after the tornado. As was the case in Joplin, there were unexpected occurrences and unexplainable dramatic details in the story. There were also notable similarities. He experienced a strong sense of peace present during and after the occurrence. The related comfort and encouragement are with him to this day.

Many years ago, a young man named, John was called into the ministry to preach when he was just 14 years old. After John's father had left his family, Pastor Raymond of their church in Columbus, Georgia, went to John's mother and asked her if it was alright for him to take John under his guidance to teach him how to pray. John looks back and describes Pastor Raymond as not just a smart man, but rather a brilliant and very humble man—probably the humblest man he has ever met in ministry. John describes Pastor Raymond as having a walk and experience with God that many people would envy. John was standing near his mother when Pastor Raymond asked her and thought to himself, "I was not called to pray. I was called to preach."

John now recognizes that Pastor Raymond knew if John was ever going to be successful, he had to develop a prayer life, because his success would come out of prayer not out of preaching. John says that in the Christian world today, success is not acquired through the glamour or talents that we see, it is born out of prayer. Prayer is the key.

John went into those prayer meetings with Pastor Raymond with a sense of awe, because he recognized the pastor as being such a man of God. Though, there were some nights that John sat there bored. He sometimes wondered what he was doing there with this old man in these nightly "Midnight Prayer Meetings." Pastor Raymond and John would gather with other men from the church after those men's shifts at the nearby mills and foundries ended. The men would take their shoes off, then join together in prayer. On some nights, there might be 12 to 15 men. On other nights, there may be 30. On many nights, there were only two—Pastor Raymond and John.

John went to the church to pray with Pastor Raymond every night for over two years.

John used to think about those prayer meetings and wonder what he was doing there. He would go to the baseball fields at night and see the other teenage boys out there playing, their family and friends in the stands watching the games. John would say to himself, "What am I doing? Here I am, in a prayer meeting." As he looks back today, John says, "Oh, how I thank God for those prayer meetings!"

Their church had gone into a revival with an evangelist at one time. John remembers that it was a bad situation. The revival went on for about 6 to 8 weeks before it came to a head. Pastor Raymond went to the evangelist and told him that he did not know what it was, but there was something there that was definitely wrong with the evangelist. He could not quite put his finger on it, but something in the evangelist's life was definitely not right. Pastor Raymond let the evangelist know that he was going to close the revival down because there was something in his spirit, something in his heart, that instinctively told him something was wrong.

The evangelist threw a fit. He knew that there were people in the church who agreed with him and recognized that he drew large crowds. He ended up causing Pastor Raymond a lot of grief and a lot of heartache. John, now 15 years old, saw the effect that this trouble had on the pastor as he went through the ordeal. It was the first sign of "church trouble" John ever remembered witnessing. John recalls seeing his first petition circulated by a student in high school to get rid of Pastor Raymond. John saw how sinister the evangelist was in his dealings with Pastor Raymond and the church. The evangelist had people working, trying to get rid of Pastor Raymond so that he could continue to stay there for the revival.

It was later discovered that the evangelist had a police record of inappropriate behavior with children at previous revivals. He had been caught, tried, found guilty, and put in jail for those offenses. After he had gotten out of jail, he resumed his work as an evangelist, ending up in John's church. The evangelist was later caught for the same behavior and was again put back into jail. John cannot understand how the church members, even after Pastor Raymond was found to be correct in his dealings with the evangelist, did not rally behind the pastor. The evangelist had been caught, and the blame was true, yet Pastor Raymond still experienced the brunt of it. They still stood against the pastor.

It ended up splitting the church in two. The church membership dropped by about two-thirds, from 300 people to just over 100. John remembers the services having a very heavy tone.

John had gone with some of the other teenagers and Pastor Raymond to get a bite to eat at a café about 10 p.m. one Sunday night after church. After they had ordered their hamburgers, the pastor leaned across the table to tell the boys that he was "going to be leaving the church." John was devastated because Pastor Raymond, who had taken the place of John's father, had become such a large part of his life. Afterwards, the group went to the church to pray, John feeling withdrawn.

Drawing away from the rest of the prayer group, John went out and sat in the middle section of the audience seats in the church by himself. Incredibly upset, he just wanted to go home and get away from everything, but the buses in Columbus ran every night except Sunday and it was too far to walk. He had no way to get home. He felt like he was stuck there. He now thanks God that he was; John could have missed one of the most important nights of his life.

The men in the group that night walked around the church sanctuary praying. After about 20 minutes or so of praying, John saw Pastor Raymond move from the back corner of the church and head toward the front. Within just a few minutes, all 17 of those there that Sunday night, including John, had made their way to the front of the church and sat on the altar benches.

While they were sitting there, a strange hush came into

the church building. The two huge metal doors in the back of the sanctuary were only used on Sundays and Wednesdays. The massive doors were securely locked—pins in the jambs at the top of the doors and bottom of the doors, a deadbolt, a key, and a latch. All of a sudden, something hit those doors with such power that they literally flew open, yet the metal knobs barely touched the plaster walls behind them before they stopped. There was no damage to the doors, latches, or walls.

In from the porch outside those doors walked one angel, the biggest creature that John had ever seen in his life. That large angel came in and walked to where Pastor Raymond had always prayed, in the back left-hand corner of the church. The angel turned and just stood there, facing toward the front of the church. In behind this angel walked another angel from the porch. The second angel came in and walked to the back right-hand corner of the church, turned, and stood facing the front of the church. The angels just stood there like soldiers with their hands at their sides.

John noticed that the huge angel on the right was standing next to a bookcase that John used as part of the church library. He had needed a ladder to place books on the top shelf, but recalls that, as the angel stood next to the bookcase, it looked like a little matchbox. All 17 of those sitting quietly on the altar benches saw the angels. The men never addressed the angels. The angels never addressed the men. The angels did not have wings. They were just stalwart, huge beings. John remembers seeing a little aura about their head and shoulders as they stood. Their presence just filled the back of that church from the top to the bottom. They never moved their lips. They never moved their bodies.

John—at 15 years of age—had been praying with Pastor Raymond and the other men for about one and a half years. As John sat there, he remembered looking at those angels on both sides of the building thinking, "My God! Jesus! Wow! Look at that." There was not much that he was able to say. He remembered thinking that "this is big boy stuff. I am too young for this." The back doors of the church were still standing wide open. Periodically, John would see the headlights and taillights of cars that passed by.

After they stood there for what seemed like just a few minutes, the first angel turned very soldier-like toward the middle of the church and walked to the center aisle. It then turned very soldier-like toward the open back door and walked out onto the porch and disappeared into the darkness of the night. The second angel did the same thing. The doors were still standing wide open after the angels had left the building.

Pastor Raymond did not seem unusually moved. Without saying a word, Pastor Raymond stood up from the altar bench and started to walk toward the back of the church to close the doors. The other 16 jumped up and got in behind the pastor as he walked toward the open doors. Unsure of what might happen next, John got as close to Pastor Raymond as he could.

The group moved closer to the back of the church where the angels had stood, but the men never made it all the way to the open doors. For, as the men reached the area where the angels had been standing, there was so much of the power of God that they fell to the floor, stacked up like firewood in the center aisle.

At 7 a.m. on Monday morning, the doors were still open, a reminder of their angelic visitors the night before. The sun shone through the doors onto that pile of men still stacked on the floor. They all awakened around the same time that morning —many hours after the angels had left.

On Wednesday night, the church was packed. The church had never been crowded on Wednesday nights. John guesses that people had heard about the angels in the church three nights earlier.

Nothing unusual happened that Wednesday night until Pastor Raymond said to "bow your heads for the offering." When he prayed over the offering, 38 people fell out of their seats onto the floor and received the Baptism of the Holy Spirit.

The back of the "church trouble" had been broken that Sunday night and not another echo of it returned.

◆ ◆ ◆

"Do not forget or neglect or refuse to extend hospitality to strangers [in the brotherhood—being friendly, cordial, and gracious, sharing the comforts of your home and doing your part generously], for through it some have entertained angels without knowing it."—**Hebrews 13:2 (AMPC)**

This story also presented itself during our interview phase. It occurred just a few years prior near Seneca, Missouri, about 10 miles south of Joplin. There are several details of this particular story that stand out. We may not recognize anything unusual at first. We may not expect anything to happen. We may not appreciate the extraordinary within events until we have time to reflect on the details. Yet, unbeknownst to us, God's Hand is in everything.

Anita was on her way home from her store after having finished working for the day. She planned to stop to make a deposit at the bank in Seneca, Missouri. The weather that day was lousy. It was pouring rain, as it had done steadily for the 3 days prior, and the forecast still promised another 3 to 4 days of the same.

It was about 5:30 p.m. on that late spring day when she noticed that there was a young, black gentleman pushing his bicycle north on the shoulder of the road. She did not stop her car as it was pouring down rain and she had to get to the bank before they closed. On her way home from the bank, she drove past the same gentleman, who was now traveling south—the opposite direction of when she saw him last.

Anita felt that there was something very unusual about this gentleman. She pulled her car over to talk to him. When she asked him where he was going, he answered, "Chicago," which happened to be her hometown. What a coincidence. She told the gentleman that it was supposed to rain continuously for the next three days and that he could stay at her home until she and her husband, David, could make arrangements to get him to Chicago the next day. They put his bicycle in the trunk and the gentleman walked around and slipped into the passenger seat, clothes dry despite the pouring rain. When she asked his name, he told her it was Michael.

She stopped by the grocery store before she headed home to get some hot dogs and chili for dinner that night. Michael stayed in the car while Anita shopped. She called David to tell him that she was bringing someone home for dinner. Michael was very quiet, not talking too much on the way. She thought at first that he might be homeless. When she asked where he was coming from, Michael answered, "California." Anita thought that it was a little odd because she had some family members from California as well. When they arrived at her house, Anita helped him place his bicycle in the garage to keep it dry. Anita noticed that even in the midst of this continual deluge of rain, his clothes were not wet. It was now nearly nightfall.

After dinner, Anita, David, and Michael sat on the couch. She could not remember if Michael had actually eaten anything. There was a Christian church service/program on the television as they sat there in the living room. As the program progressed, Michael would lean back in the chair from time to time. He would smile and shake his head occasionally as he watched. Anita asked Michael if the program on the television was bothering him. Michael replied, "No. No. No. It is not right." Anita thought that the answer seemed a little bit odd, but did not give it much consideration.

As Anita talked to Michael, he said that he had not been to Chicago in a long time. She offered to wash his clothes while he took a shower, but Michael told her that his clothes were fine and would not need washing. Anita showed Michael where his room and everything was in case he needed to get up in the middle of the night. She told him to help himself to the food in the refrigerator. He told her that he would not be hungry. Anita still thought that Michael was a homeless person.

Anita woke up in the middle of the night and was walking down the hallway when she noticed the light was on in Michael's room and the door was open a bit. She looked in and saw Michael sitting on the floor reading the Bible. She made sure that he was alright and assured Michael that he could sleep in the bed. He assured her that he was alright and really didn't sleep very much. He continued to read the Bible throughout the night.

She was still trying to figure out why he was there in Seneca on his way to Chicago, 600 or so miles away. She was intrigued why he was going two different directions on his bicycle at two different times, while on his way to the same place. She could not understand how his clothes could have possibly stayed dry as she took him out of a driving rain that afternoon. Earlier on, David had asked Anita if she thought Michael was going to be alright. She told him that she thought he would be fine and felt no anxiety about having him in the house. They had welcomed strangers into their home before. She would later say it felt different this time. She almost felt like he was an angel.

When David got up to go to work the next morning, it was still pouring down rain as it had done all night. Michael told Anita he would have to leave soon. She said there would be no way that he could leave on his bicycle in the deluge. They would go to the bus station to buy Michael a ticket to Chicago and get the bicycle boxed up to take on the bus. Anita hurried to the store to see if she could get a box for the bicycle and prepared sandwiches and a thermos of milk for Michael to take with him.

At the bus depot, Anita gave Michael his bus ticket and sack lunch for the trip. The attendants loaded the box with the bicycle into the luggage compartment underneath the floor of the bus. Michael gave Anita a hug and said, "Bless you." Anita gave him their phone numbers before he walked around the front of the bus to climb aboard. Michael assured Anita that he knew where they lived and how to get a hold of her. As soon as he left her, Anita checked her pockets and found some spare dollar bills and walked around to give them to Michael before the bus left. When she got to the front of the bus, she could not find him. She walked down the side of the bus to look into the windows and could not see him inside. He was nowhere to be found. It was as if he was just gone. She went home with a strong sense of peace that had overcome her.

Anita's sister-in-law had been pregnant at the time. She was having some complications with the pregnancy and was planning on staying with Anita for a while. While she was in their home, she stayed in the same room where Michael had stayed. Her sister-in-law sat where Michael sat on the couch and commented one evening that she felt such a strong sense of peace present in the house. Despite the trials that would occur, that strong sense of peace would never leave.

CHAPTER 4
ANGELS IN THE STORM

"For He will give His angels [especial] charge over you to accompany and defend and preserve you in all your ways [of obedience and service]."—**Psalm 91:11 (AMPC)**

"Bless the LORD, you His angels, who excel in strength, who do His word, heeding the voice of His word. Bless the LORD, all you His hosts, you ministers of His, who do His pleasure."—**Psalm 103:20-21 (NKJV)**

"Are not the angels all ministering spirits (servants) sent out in the service [of God for the assistance] of those who are to inherit salvation?"—**Hebrews 1:14 (AMPC)**

E verybody in the Joplin, Missouri area remembers what occurred on the evening of Sunday, May 22, 2011. They know where they were, what they were doing, where they were going, and who was with them. The events of that evening are seared into their memories.

The days and weeks afterward were qualified by words such as damage, loss, injury, debris, destruction, and death. They were described with terms such as panic, fear, chaos, anxiety, sorrow, and grief. It was heart-wrenching to see storm survivors digging through piles of rubble of what had once been their homes, looking for a trinket, cherished photo, or memento that would give them some degree of comfort.

When one would travel through the neighborhoods, there was an imbalance that became noticeable. The tally of approximately 1,300 treated injuries and the 161 deaths did not seem to correlate with the destruction or near destruction of 6,000 to 8,000 homes, 550 businesses, including over 100 medical offices, 1 regional medical center, 27 churches, 10 children's daycare facilities, 3 nursing homes, 28 apartment complexes, and approximately 18,000 vehicles. Four thousand utility poles with hundreds of miles of electrical, telephone, and cable wire needed to be replaced as well as 30 manhole covers. When you looked at any of those homes, you could not help but wonder how or where any person could have survived. One statistic we tracked was the number of people who lived inside the city limits and were displaced by the storm. The number of people whose homes were unlivable because of the storm, whether for a period of just a few days or up to permanent displacement, was over 35 percent. More than one third of the city was rendered homeless due to this storm. There were theories that the number of casualties and injuries were not being reported for various reasons. Many people believed that there was simply no possible way that the loss of life could be so low. Only by the grace of God, were there not 500 or 1,000 who lost their lives on that late spring day.

Then the stories began to come out. There were accounts of things that happened that just did not seem right. One person noted that, "something just told them to go into one room of their home instead of another and that the room chosen was all that was left of the building." Many felt as if they were guided toward a specific room or maybe even to a precise spot. One mother described how her "son knelt down on the floor next to his hot water heater near the outside wall of his home. The wind blew the wall down, knocking him and the hot water heater to the floor as the house collapsed over him. The void on the floor next to the hot water heater was all the space that he needed for protection from the collapsed house above him, and it was the only place in the rubble that was large enough to hold him." Another person, and another, and another, and countless more would tell the story of where they sought protection from the storm's fury as it pounded their home or business. When the storm subsided, they recounted that all that remained of their home or business was the precise spot where they were located. It was not always the hall, or the closet, or the bathroom, or the pantry. It was just merely the space where they found shelter.

Then there were more stories, and more stories, and more stories, all different, yet the same.

There were accounts of unexplainable, unidentified people who were helping those in need, all across the city. The person would be present one moment, and then gone the next. Some of the descriptions of these helpers were consistently unusual in relation to the events and surroundings. Many people began to describe items that were miraculously available to allow them protection from the fury of the storm. One such person recounts that, "the car that was hurled into the basement where we were taking shelter just miraculously barely missed us. The ladder that ended up next to it allowed us to climb out of the basement to safety." For some "unexplained reason," there was just the right item at precisely the right time that showed up exactly where it was needed to allow further protection or escape.

Other people became aware of some seemingly random, well-placed items that remained in view after the winds destroyed everything around; items that would serve as a reminder to them that they were protected. The items were very prominent in the massive piles of debris scattered everywhere. It would be amazing if just one story had surfaced. It would be that much more so if there were 2 or 3 stories. How amazing would 5 such stories be? How about 10 stories? How about 20 stories? How about 50 stories? In just the small number of people we talked to firsthand, there were between 50 and 100 stories. How many more amazing stories from people are out there who we never had the chance to interview? Even though this is just a small sample of recollections, I would believe that it is highly probable that there are hundreds or more of these testimonies still being recounted across the city.

Almost all the people interviewed described an incredibly strong sense of peace, comfort, or warmth that felt as if it was enveloping them as their world disintegrated around them. Some children began to tell of seeing "women with wings," "butterflies," or "angels" who would protect them or their family members.

As the stories began to pour in, it became very evident that there were many similarities among the different stories. As we tried to group them together, it also became very obvious that many of the stories had multiple facets that would allow them to be categorized into groups. We have arranged these people with their stories into the following groups:

1) People who were in **THE RIGHT PLACE AT THE RIGHT TIME**.
2) People who felt the **POWER AND PRESENCE OF GOD** around them.
3) People who saw and felt **GOD's PROTECTION** around them.
4) People who received **GUIDANCE AND DIRECTION** through the storm.
5) People who received **COMFORT** during the storm.
6) People who received changes in their **HEALTH** during and immediately after the storm.
7) People who witnessed an individual presented in a timely manner to assist and/or comfort them. The individual in one unannounced moment was with them **HERE, THEN GONE** in an instant when their task was completed.
8) People who **BUTTERFLIES**—BUTTERFLY PEOPLE.
9) People who felt a strong sense of **GOD'S PEACE** around them during and immediately after the storm.
10) People who recognized CHANCE OCCURENCES and

UNEXPLAINABLE SIGNS during and after the storm, that affirmed to them the EVIDENCE OF GOD'S HAND and provide them with much needed **HOPE**.

As you read them, you will recognize that a number of these firsthand testimonies cross into several different groups. The stories are arranged in each of these groups in order from west to east, as the storm traveled across the city.

(The following maps were produced by the U.S. Army Corps of Engineers; 2011)

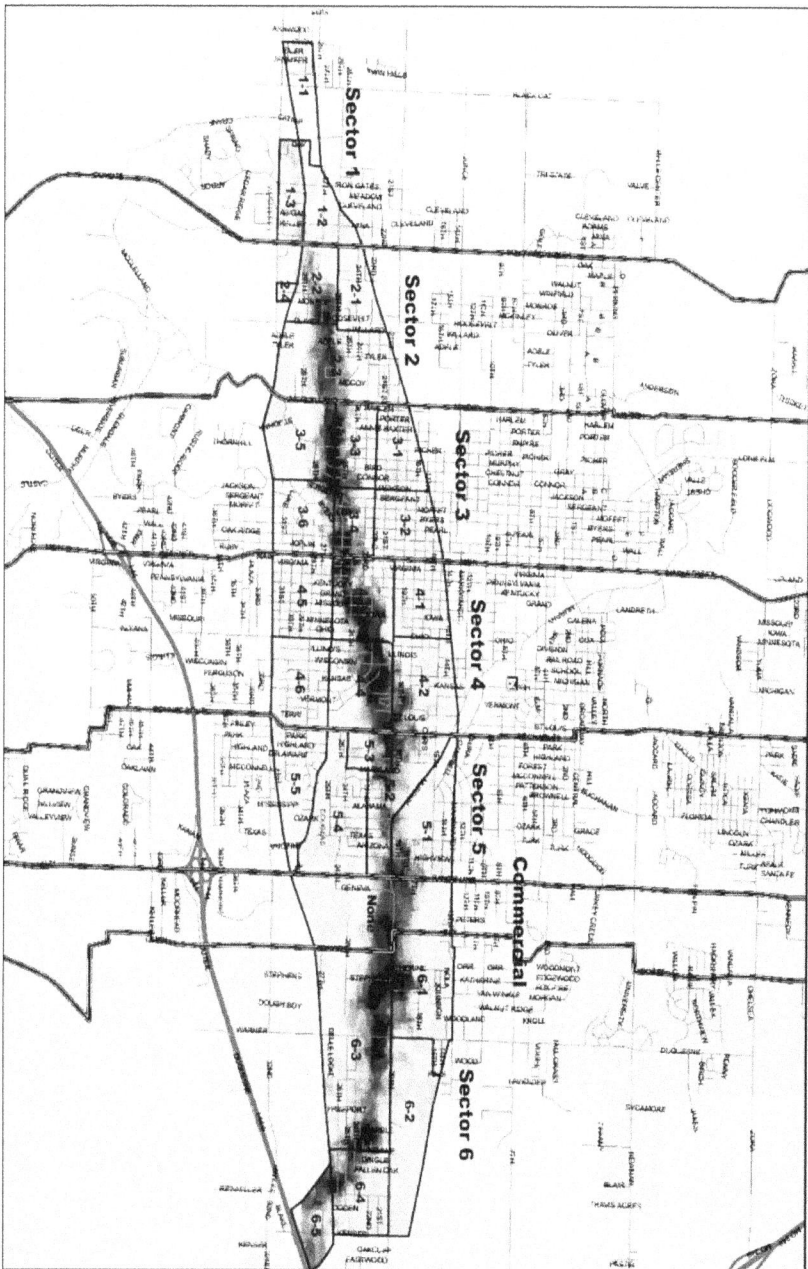

JOPLIN MISSOURI ESTIMATED STRUCTURE DAMAGE - 5 JUNE 2011

JOPLIN MISSOURI TORNADO PATH IMPACTED AREA

Legend

USACE - RFO

Structure Damage

Catastrophic Damage

Moderate Damage

Location Map

CHAPTER 5
DEVELOPMENT AND
CLASSIFICATION OF TORNADOES

G enerally, in the Midwest, tornadoes are formed when unstable, moist air moving north from the Gulf of Mexico collides with much colder air above or in the jet stream. This collision causes severe disturbances in the atmosphere and a resulting low-pressure area at the ground. The air surrounding the low-pressure area is drawn in to fill that void. As the air rushes in and is pulled up into a chimney, a spinning effect in the air results. Usually, the air moving toward the chimney rotates counterclockwise around the chimney and ascends into the chimney, becoming a twisting column of potentially violent wind.

Stronger tornadoes are usually found close to the edge of the updraft in a thunderstorm, not far from where the air is descending. Falling rain or hail can pull down that colder upper air to form downdrafts or increase the air flow in already present downdrafts. There may be a burst of heavy rain or a hail storm in close proximity to a tornado.

The funnel cloud of a tornado may be nearly transparent or white until dust and/or debris are picked up, or a cloud forms inside the funnel. Most tornadoes are likely to form between 3 p.m. and 9 p.m., during the heat of the day, but can form anytime. The average tornado moves from southwest to northeast. The average forward speed of a tornado is 30 miles per hour but may reach speeds of 70 miles per hour. Most tornadoes occur east of the Rocky Mountains during the spring and summer months.

Tornado severity is ranked on the "F Scale" created by Tetsuya Theodore Fujita at the University of Chicago. The wind speed and severity of a tornado is estimated by the damage caused. The limits and descriptions of the different "F Scale" classifications, as well as their frequency of occurrence, according to the "Tornado Project Online," are described as follows:

An **"F-0: Gale Tornado"** has winds that range from 40 to 72 miles per hour. These winds can cause damage to some fireplace chimneys and sign boards, may break branches off trees and topple shallow rooted trees.

An **"F-1: Moderate Tornado"** has winds that range from 73 to 112 miles per hour. These winds can damage roofs. The winds may pull mobile homes from their foundations or even overturn them. The winds may push cars off road surfaces or destroy attached garages. The F-0 and F-1 tornadoes are considered weak. Of all the tornadoes recorded between 1950 and 1994, 74 percent of them were measured as F-0 or F-1.

An **"F-2: Significant Tornado"** has winds that range between 113 and 157 miles per hour. The winds can cause considerable amounts of damage. They can tear roofs from light-frame houses. Mobile homes may be demolished, and railroad boxcars can be overturned. Large trees will be snapped or uprooted. The winds can lift cars off the ground and light objects can turn into projectiles.

An **"F-3: Severe Tornado"** has winds that range between 158 and 206 miles per hour. The winds can tear roofs and walls off well-constructed houses and are strong enough to throw cars and overturn entire trains. The powerful winds can uproot most trees, even trees in a forest area. From 1950 to 1994, 25 percent of all tornadoes recorded were considered strong tornadoes, F-2 or F-3.

An **"F-4: Devastating Tornado"** has destructive winds that range between 207 and 260 miles per hour. Most homes, even well-constructed homes, may be leveled or destroyed. Some structures with weak foundations may be blown long distances. Large objects are turned into projectiles.

An **"F-5: Incredible Tornado"** has destructive winds that range between 261 and 318 miles per hour. The force of the winds can lift and blow well-constructed houses off their foundations or can disintegrate well-constructed homes. Cars are thrown more than 100 meters. Steel-reinforced concrete buildings are badly damaged. Trees will be de-barked. The force of the wind can cause incredible phenomena to occur. F-4 and F-5 tornadoes, called violent tornadoes, account for only 1 percent of all recorded tornadoes from 1950 to 1994. Very few F-5 tornadoes occur.

An **"F-6: Inconceivable Tornado"** has winds greater than 318 miles per hour. These winds may be possible but have never been documented. The storms are considered inconceivable. It would be difficult to measure such a tornado as there would likely be no objects left to study. Any further higher classification of the current measuring scale would be a hypothetical modification.

CHAPTER 6
JOPLIN HISTORY OF TORNADOES

The May 22, 2011, tornado that cut a swath from one city limit to the other was the worst tornado to hit Joplin, Missouri but it was not the first. According to an article titled *"Twisters, Cyclones and Tornadoes of Joplin's Past: Part 1"* found on the "Historic Joplin" website, there were two smaller tornadoes that struck the city of Joplin, Missouri near the beginning of the 20th century. The records describe a small tornado in May 1883. A more serious tornado struck in April 1902. With damage reported between 13th Street and 16th Street from Moffett Avenue to Bird Avenue and from Main Street to Grand Avenue, between 7th Street and 9th Street. Property damage was estimated at $50,000, with 50 to 60 houses destroyed. There was a small funnel that struck some mining camps in Joplin, Missouri in the summer of 1908. It was small enough that only one of the city's newspapers found it noteworthy to mention even a brief report of the incident. In the spring of 1911, another powerful windstorm found its way between north Joplin and south Webb City, Missouri, after leaving a path of destruction through Oklahoma and Kansas.

An article in the Joplin Globe titled *"Brad Belk: May tornadoes struck Joplin twice in the 1970's"* dated May 8, 2010, detailed and compared two previous storms from the early 1970's. In a span of just 2 years, there were two destructive tornadoes that touched down in Joplin, Missouri, both in the month of May. On May 5, 1971, at about 5 p.m., a tornado touched down near 26th Street and Schifferdecker Avenue and began its 40-block trek through the center of Joplin. It stayed on the ground, crossing Main Street near 12th Street, finally dissipating near Missouri Southern State College. The storm took 1 life, injured 60 people, damaged more than 1,500 homes, and caused $20 million in damage.

Two years later, on the morning of May 11, 1973, an early morning "tornadic windstorm" struck the city. The 70 to 100 mile per hour winds out of the northwest battered the city. There were 3 lives lost and more than 100 injured. About 100 homes were damaged. More than 1,000 trees were uprooted or broken. Sixty families were displaced. The storm caused more than $12.8 million dollars in damage.

More recently, Joplin experienced several incidents associated with microbursts or "gustnados," caused by severe downdrafts. Damage was minimal and no loss of life was recorded in those incidences.

On May 22, 2011, at about 5:30 p.m., Joplin's history with windstorms and tornadoes would be forever and dramatically changed.

CHAPTER 7
MAY 22, 2011

A llen, with 4 States Search and Rescue, remembers the storm chasers who were in town that day following this particular storm. Mike Bettes, with The Weather Channel, was tracking the storm from the southern side. He was coming up I-44 with his crew. Jeff Piotrowski, a professional storm chaser, was coming into Joplin, Missouri from the northwest. He drove west on 7th Street with his wife, Kathryn. Jeff and Kathryn were monitoring the development of the huge storm forming in the southwest portion of the city. They noticed a Joplin Police Department officer working as a storm spotter stationed near Carousel Park on West 7th Street and notified the officer of a "rain-wrapped monster" that had very quickly developed about 2 miles south of their location. Piotrowski urged the officer to sound a storm warning siren, the "second siren," that caught many people's attention.

At noon, Allen's wife, Alicia, had gotten onto the storm spotter network—the websites use GPS to track the location of the crews in real time. That afternoon, Alicia had called Allen to let him know they should probably keep a closer watch on the weather. She told Allen there were a number of storm chasers eating lunch at the Denny's at the Flying J Travel Center. Allen is not a big social network person, but he knew that The Weather Channel was using Twitter—he signed up for Twitter that day. He saw many Tweets going out early that afternoon mentioning Joplin as the target of a major storm, long before the storm had even begun to fire up.

May 22 seemed like any other late spring Sunday in Joplin. Some people were getting ready to head to evening church services. Some people were listening to the I-70 Series baseball game between the St. Louis Cardinals and the Kansas City Royals on the radio. Some families were on their way to the Joplin High School graduation ceremony at the Leggett and Platt Athletic Center on the campus of Missouri Southern State University. Others were just relaxing at home. There was a moderate risk of severe weather forecasted for the Joplin area. The risk of thunderstorm had been upgraded from a slight risk of severe thunderstorm just two days prior.

If there is a tornado or severe weather in Jasper or Newton counties in Missouri—which Joplin is a part of—or Cherokee County in southeast Kansas, and the projected path of those storms crosses any portion of the city limits of Joplin, the storm warning sirens are sounded. The warning sirens are sounded regardless of the size of the storm. The warning sirens are also activated if a significant storm is either sighted visually or detected on radar.

The weather forecast for that day and the few days prior was nothing out of the ordinary for that time of year in Joplin. There were forecasts of thunderstorms and tornado watches for much of the area, including notable strong circulation approaching from the west. By 4 p.m., the storms forming in southeast Kansas were starting to garner more attention. Severe thunderstorms began to rapidly increase in strength with the possibility for more serious weather.

There was another storm cell developing just north and west of Joplin that very quickly began to display circulation and strong updrafts. There were reports from Cherokee County, Kansas of strong winds and hail. There was also a report of a wall cloud in Cherokee county—the presence of a wall cloud can lead to the formation of a tornado. The storm warning sirens for

Joplin and the surrounding area were sounded about 5:15 p.m., then stopped a few minutes later.

The two powerful storm cells were on a merger or collision course headed directly toward Joplin, with strong circulation present in both storms. The Joplin Police Department officer, stationed as a storm spotter near Carousel Park on West 7th Street, was urged by Jeff Piotrowski to sound the storm warning sirens. Jeff saw the massive rain-wrapped storm cell on his radar screen forming near the southwest corner of Joplin. The second storm warning siren, sounding just shortly after 5:30 p.m., caught many people's attention in the city. The people were used to and almost oblivious to the warning sirens that would sound periodically through the spring and summer. This siren was different though and many people became much more aware. The siren was not an indication of the size or strength of the storm, but rather just that the storm was there.

The collision, or merger, of the two storm cells occurred near 27th Street and Schifferdecker Avenue near Joplin's western limits. The relatively low strength of each storm escalated higher once they merged into one. There were reports of several vortices circulating about the monster that made its way through the city.

There was collateral damage from this tornado that, in some locations, stretched nearly 1 mile on either side of the center of the direct path. This storm was described as traveling much slower than the average tornado as it "camped out and crawled" across the city at the slow pace of only about 25 miles per hour. The National Weather Service says the storm may have advanced as slowly as 10 miles per hour in some places. While that sounds very slow, the front wall of the storm at only 20 miles per hour advances 1 city block in just less than 10 seconds. When people saw the storm bearing down on them, they had only seconds to react. The longest period of time for any of the persons interviewed to react, once they realized that the storm was imminent until the front wall of the storm physically reached them, was 30 seconds. Most people had much less. Some had no warning at all. The rain-wrapped wall advancing on them appeared to stretch 5 to 6 blocks to either side. There simply was nowhere to go to escape the fury of the storm and not enough time to get out of the way.

CHAPTER 8
TIMELINE OF THE STORM

T his story is a little different in its content than the stories to follow. It is from an individual who rode out the storm inside a walk-in cooler at the Fastrip convenience store on the corner of 20th Street and Duquesne Road. He had turned on the video recorder on his cell phone just before the storm struck the building and captured video and audio of the storm as it raged overhead. It was a miracle that all 23 people in the cooler survived with only minor injuries as the storm scored a direct hit on the building. The video timeline allows the viewer to observe the order and sequence of events as they were recorded in real time, objectively, without the distortion of subjective human emotion and perception.

Shortly after 5:15 p.m., a friend was driving around Joplin running some errands and listening to the I-70 Series baseball game between the St. Louis Cardinals and the Kansas City Royals on the radio with two of his friends. As they were driving, they could hear the tornado warning sirens. Like almost everyone else in Joplin who heard those first sirens, they did not pay too much attention. The storm warning sirens almost never precede an actual damaging storm.

By about the 5th inning, the three friends listened as the weather updates began breaking in on the baseball game broadcast. The reports started to become a constant interruption on the AM station out of Kansas. They decided to switch over to a local FM station to get a better idea of what was causing all the alerts.

Weather announcers mentioned something about the evacuation or early dismissal of the Joplin High School graduation ceremonies that were in progress at the Leggett and Platt Athletic Center on the campus of Missouri Southern State University. They drove by the campus to see what was happening there. The report from the radio station mentioned that the power had gone out and the station was relying on an emergency back-up generator. The station's access to the radar and computers for storm tracking and monitoring was limited due to the loss of power.

By the time the trio reached the intersection of Duquesne Road and Newman Road, the rain began to intensify. They turned south on Duquesne Road to head back into town. By about 5:40 p.m. they had reached the intersection of 7th Street and Duquesne Road. Weather reports indicated that a tornado had been spotted on the ground at 7th Street and Range Line Road, about one and a half miles east of their location. The sky was getting much darker and the overall weather conditions had gone from bad to worse in just a matter of minutes. The trio reasoned that the best way to get out of the path of a tornado was to go directly north or south of the path. If the tornado was seen at 7th Street and Range Line Road, the campus at Missouri Southern State University was closer to the possible path of the storm. Turning around and going back north would just take them closer to the tornado. They thought they could get farther away from the path by heading straight south towards 20th Street and beyond. They did not know the storm that was spotted from 7th Street and Range Line Road was actually about a mile farther south at 20th Street. They had no idea they were heading directly into the center of the storm's path. It was now 5:45 p.m. and the storm was on its march through the city of Joplin.

They had initially planned on driving west on 20th Street to the Sonic Drive-In on Range Line Road to escape the tremendous rain and hail that they were now experiencing. As they approached the corner of 20th Street, the rain was coming down in sheets. They were unaware that the storm they saw was indeed the tornado. They were planning to turn west on 20th Street and realized that the weather was much worse than they had expected, and was intensifying rapidly.

By the time they reached 20th Street on Duquesne Road, one of them noticed the rotation of the clouds in the front wall of the storm looming to the west and advancing on them quickly. They knew they had to get out of the car. They decided against the Sonic Drive-In option. They saw the Fastrip store at the corner of 20th Street and Duquesne Road as their last and only hope of getting into a substantial structure that would afford them some protection from the storm. The rain was falling almost horizontally to the ground as they pulled into the parking lot. The sky had darkened. The power had gone out by the time they reached the intersection. They pulled up right in front of the store and ran to the door. The door was locked but the manager quickly let the three men inside. They followed the manager to the back wall of the store near the walk-in cooler where there was already a group of 16 people taking refuge. Within the next minute, there would also be a father and his three children pounding on the locked front door to get in. They would be the last of the 23 people and 1 little dog who would arrive to ride out the storm.

On this day, this friend turned on the recorder of his cell phone and pointed the lens toward the front door. By now, the sky visible from their spot in the back of the store had gone from a dark grayish green to almost pitch black. The canopies above the gas pumps outside were flapping up and down in the steadily increasing winds like giant wings. The front face of the storm was less than 2 blocks away. Before long, the sky outside had become so dark that the recorded video image recorded would seem to pick up just noises and voices as it still continued to record the unfolding events. As the darkness increased, the noise level throughout the storm increased dramatically as well.

The phone continued recording the video and audio of the storm for the next 5 minutes. At the two-and-a-half-minute mark amidst the chaos and confusion, he had completely forgotten about the phone, but the video and audio continued recording. There were several notable items of this particular recording that are pertinent to the stories in this book. The most important result is that there were 23 people who sought shelter inside the safety of the store and all 23 people, and the Dachshund, survived, suffering only minor injuries. The other information that we get from this recording is an accurate and objective timeline of events at that location. The video and audio recordings are objective. They are not based on or affected by a personal subjective experience. The objective timeline is not affected by the human perception of time that could seem to slow down or speed up to be compressed. By using the timeline on this recording, we are able to get a more accurate idea of the timeline that others in the storm might have experienced.

From the video, you can hear the responses from the people as the rear wall of the store—just behind where they had sought refuge—began to move and bow in and out from the force of the destructive wind. The bottles began to rattle and crack.

The preceding wind gusts ahead of the storm smashed into the store just 45 seconds after the father and his three children made it inside. The sound was incredibly loud as the windows on the front face of the store exploded. With those windows and doors now gone, much of the store's inventory was sucked out through the openings into the darkness outside. The store filled with a dense blackness as the storm passed directly overhead. By now, the manager had begun to herd everybody into the walk-in cooler.

Thirty-five seconds later, the front face of the storm

smashed into the building. People were still working amid the chaos and darkness to get everybody into the cooler; they were pelted with debris as they made their way in. It took only about 45 seconds for the last person to reach the new, relative safety of the walk-in cooler.

Before the manager could latch the door of the cooler, the loosened front facade of the store was pulled away from the last attachment to the building and launched into the black sky. A heavy object or the force of the wind slammed the cooler door shut.

The walk-in cooler measured about 25 feet long, by 8 feet wide, by 7 feet high on the outside. Because there were two suspended air conditioning units and heavy industrial shelves inside the cooler, the refuge was confining for the 23 people inside—but there was no other viable alternative.

The audio of the recording allows you to hear the roar of the wind outside, the sound of metal creaking and twisting, and wood splintering and cracking. The intense noise and blowing debris continue for 55 seconds without so much as a pause.

From the audio, it is evident that the roaring decreases as the eye of the storm rolls directly overhead. Only 55 seconds had elapsed since the front of the storm had smashed into the building. The relative calm lasted for about 25 to 30 seconds before the storm resumed it pounding on the battered store. The time was now recorded as 6 p.m.

The intensity of the back half of the storm seemed much stronger in comparison to the front half. That non-stop assault of the wind-driven debris continued for another 55 seconds. During that time, the roof of the crowded, cramped, walk-in cooler collapsed onto the people inside. The sky above had lightened to a very dark green, just a bit lighter than the black clouds that hid the front of the storm from their view. After the last 55 second run of the wind and debris, the other noises outside, probably from the intense hail that would accompany the storm, would carry on for another 20 seconds before the people finally exited through the roof of the walk-in cooler. They had to crawl out through the top of the cooler that was now leaning over to one side. The hail had stopped by the time they exited. All that was left of the store was the battered shell of the walk-in cooler.

CHAPTER 9
CASUALTY PROJECTIONS

Like many other people in Joplin, Missouri on that Sunday in May, Rusty, an emergency medical technician (EMT), had been attending the Joplin High School graduation ceremony. As soon as the warning sirens sounded, he left the ceremony to go home where he could be closer to his radios. Arriving at his home near Cracker Barrel restaurant on south Range Line Road, he started hearing reports about the storm hitting St. John's Hospital. He began to communicate with his crews from Newton County Ambulance Service about their plan of action.

Rusty, his son, Keegan, and Jake, his future son-in law, traveled to the intersection of 20th Street and Range Line Road in an emergency vehicle about 10 minutes after the storm had gone through that area. Keegan and Jake had both been out of emergency medical technician school for about a week. The two young men had completed their training, but had not yet taken their board examinations. Two of Rusty's three daughters, Kaitlin and Shelby, both emergency room technicians—one working for Freeman Hospital and the other for St. John's Hospital—were with them as well. They set up a temporary triage area on the old 20th Street roadbed on the northeast corner of that intersection. Drawn to the emergency lights on the work vehicle, people began to gather immediately for treatment. Rusty and the group worked the triage and treatment area for 45 minutes to an hour before he was able to get an ambulance to that intersection. He was trying to find a way to get his daughters to the hospital to help there, but there were so many injured people in need of medical assistance at the triage center. While the numerous injured people were being treated, Rusty was working to size up what resources he had and what he believed he would need. He was not yet aware of the storm's scale or impact. All he knew was that there were a lot of injured people at his location.

Even though the first ambulance was finally able to reach that location about 45 minutes to an hour after they had set up triage, Rusty and the other emergency workers had already sent more than 100 injured out to Freeman Hospital by private vehicle. As soon as he was able, Rusty went up the hill to the damaged Wal-Mart store and picked up some needed blankets, comforters, and supplies to take to the triage area. There was another ambulance service at the Wal-Mart store getting the last of the injured people out of the building.

He went over to The Home Depot parking lot and set up another triage center there. Within that first hour, 5 to 6 physicians and 6 to 7 nurses and nurse practitioners had joined the initial group. By that time, there were about 8 to 10 ambulances on site. Within the first hour, there were about 21 ambulances helping across the city. Newton County Ambulance Service had 11 ambulances and Metro Emergency Transportation Services (METS) had 10 in service across the city. About 1 hour into the emergency response, there were ambulances coming in from Springfield, Missouri, Monett, Missouri, Quapaw, Oklahoma, and other outlying areas. Before the night was over, there were more than 100 ambulances being used in the storm rescue operation.

Rusty oversaw the Southern EMS Command, south of 20th Street. METS was responsible for the Northern EMS Command, north of 20th Street. Having heard reports that there were still more storms coming or possibly more tornadoes to develop through the evening, Rusty asked the crew from Quapaw Fire Department to see if the damaged Walgreen's building on the corner of 20th Street and Range Line Road could be used to get some of the injured people out of the weather. The fire crew reported that the building was unsafe. With enough medical personnel at The Home Depot triage and treatment center, Rusty went to the Fletcher Toyota dealership on 24th Street and Range Line Road to see if the garages at the car dealership could be used for emergency treatment in the case of more storms. While there was less damage in that building, it was still too much, and the downed power lines posed even more problems. Rusty ended up at Lowe's, a couple of blocks further south. There was generator back-up and power available at Lowe's, so they ended up transferring the triage and treatment center to that location. It was between 10 p.m. and 11 p.m. when the triage and treatment center was finally set up.

Rusty was finally able to make it to the Emergency Operations Center in the basement of Fire Station #1 at the old, downtown City Hall building by midnight. Rusty, the Joplin fire chief, and the METS administrator were able to meet to assess and review rescue operations. They projected that, considering the widespread damage and destruction, they expected the fatality count would be somewhere between 300 and 500 by the time the sun would come up. Those numbers would then expectedly increase over the days following. Even at that point in time, they had no idea of the full extent of the damage.

Rusty was told that the Disaster Medical Assistance Team (DMAT) was enroute from St. Louis, Missouri, and Branson, Missouri, with a liaison at Freeman Hospital, so he traveled to Freeman to help get that group set up. The DMAT was eventually set up at the old Ford dealership building on 31st Street and Range Line Road. Any ambulances that came into town from the south and east would report to the DMAT staging area at the 31st Street and Range Line Road location. Any ambulances that came into Joplin from the north and west would report to the Northern EMS Command staging area at the METS office at 6th Street and Virginia Avenue. The Joplin Fire Department had its staging area at 23rd Street and Joplin Avenue, on the parking lot of the old South Middle School. The triage treatment area at Lowe's would be transitioned to the DMAT location by about 6 a.m. the next morning.

Rusty expected a large "second wave" of patients to come through the treatment site after rescuers were able to get into some of the more damaged areas. That "second wave" did not materialize as expected. There were a lot of people who had gone to Freeman Hospital by private vehicle or to the facility that had been set up at Memorial Hall earlier in the evening. By 11 p.m. the night of the storm, Rusty had gotten calls from Freeman Hospital and Memorial Hall. Both locations had approximately 200 total patients who had been treated and stabilized and were ready to be transferred by ambulance to facilities outside of Joplin. The out-of-town ambulances were used for out-of-town transfers, leaving the local ambulance crews in town. The ranks of over 100 ambulances in service began to thin out within 2 to 3 days. The last out-of-town ambulances stayed in town for about 10 to 14 days after the storm.

Rusty described the training preparation for such disasters. They had trained for disasters at the hospital. They had trained for disasters outside the hospital… but they had never trained for the hospital being part of the disaster itself. He said, "Shortly after the storm, there were too many people to transport and not enough available emergency personnel. The triage and treatment areas spaced at 12 block intervals, throughout the disaster zone, allowed an injured person to travel no more than 6 blocks to reach a triage and treatment site. We decided to stay in one location and treat only, allowing private vehicles to transport the less severe cases. There were only about 300 to 400 injured transported by ambulance, with the bulk of the injured transported by private vehicle."

When the sun came up Monday morning, the first casualty report came out. It listed 100 or so total fatalities, much lower than the 300 to 500 expected. Rusty was certain the numbers would rise as more of the massive debris field was searched. There were approximately 1,300 people who would be treated for storm-related injuries. Rusty believed that, based on the intense amount of destruction in such a widespread area, his predictions were still valid. Initial casualty estimates from nearby fire departments were similar. His method was not wrong, as much as there was something different in play with this storm. He felt there was no way there could be such low casualties and that it could only be attributed to the fact that God played a huge role... and nothing else.

He said, "God must have been really working overtime that day. There is no other explanation. Look at the damage and look at the low numbers of casualties. We would like to think that we had something to do with that, but it was much bigger than that."

CHAPTER 10
SEARCH AND RESCUE

Allen was at his home just south of Joplin, Missouri as the May 22, 2011 storm approached. As search and rescue professionals, he and his wife, Alicia, kept a watchful eye on the weather. They knew there was something coming but had no idea it would be as significant as it turned out to be. They did not realize Joplin was in the target zone until later in the afternoon.

As they tracked some of the storm chaser websites, it became clear that Joplin was the target of interest for numerous storm chasers. Allen and Alicia became a little more attentive to the developing weather. Allen describes it as "situational awareness." They could already see the debris cloud in the sky from their home located miles away from the actual tornado. The couple gathered their rescue animals and gear and prepared for work. Allen and Alicia own 4 States Search and Rescue. They have five working canines, trained and familiar with the demand of various natural disasters. They use three main canine handlers. One of the members was a nurse at St. John's Hospital and worked as a nurse that night. Another member of their team worked for the Jasper County Sheriff's Department and worked with the sheriff's department that night. The third member of the team volunteered with the Baxter Springs Fire Department—he worked with his dog at The GreenBriar elderly care facility, that evening.

Allen listened to some of the early eyewitness reports that were coming in on his two-way radio. There was a large tornado reported on the ground near Black Cat Road or Central City Road, just west of Joplin. One of the reports that struck a chord with Allen was when a friend, a gentleman whose voice he recognized on the radio, called in a report from 20th Street and Maiden Lane. The report mentioned a large storm that was "growing very quickly and starting to really tear things up." Allen could tell from the gentleman's voice that there was no exaggeration in the report.

Allen and Alicia did not realize how bad the storm really was until the hail began pounding them as they loaded their gear into their pickup truck and trailer. They learned that the Flying J Travel Center just a few miles away had been damaged heavily. They heard a piercing rumble as the storm churned about 1 mile north of their home. Tree branches at their home were being blown and tossed violently back and forth. Allen loaded the UTV, all-terrain vehicle, onto the trailer and tossed all their search and rescue bags into the back of the pickup truck while Alicia got the dogs ready. Hail was still pelting the ground when they headed into Joplin.

Since neither of them was officially on duty, they first went toward the west side of the city. They had some family members who lived very close to where there was a major damage area and had planned to stop by there to check on them. They had been unable to reach any of the family members by phone. They navigated their pickup truck and trailer through the debris-littered roadways on their way to 32nd Street and McClelland Boulevard. As they were approaching an intersection just south of the damaged St. John's Hospital, Allen was relieved to get a call from the grandparents whose home was near Twin Hill Country Club. They were safe and, surprisingly, not aware of what had taken place just a mile or so from their home.

When they pulled up to the intersection of 32nd Street and McClelland Boulevard, Allen looked toward St. John's Hospital just blocks to the north. For the first time in more than 25 years of public safety, he felt a sense of complete loss and helplessness.

Many people were walking around as if in a confused daze, with blank looks on their faces. Both Allen and Alicia knew how populated the area was.

They heard reports over the radio that The Home Depot had been hit. They also heard reports that Wal-Mart had been hit. They knew that Duquesne Road and the Flying J had been hit. They knew of the many apartment complexes that lined 20th Street between Indiana Avenue and Range Line Road. It was 5 p.m. on a Sunday and he believed that people would either be home watching television, or they would be shopping. With his knowledge of the area and his experience, Allen reasoned sadly that there would be no way to get through the disaster with less than 500 casualties. His first instinct was that it would be a miracle from God if there were with less than 1000 fatalities.

People's typical response to the storm warning sirens in Joplin is one of indifference, as nothing more than an ominous sky usually follows the wail of the siren. Joplin had not suffered a direct hit from a microburst or tornado in more than a decade. The last storm was very small in size, causing minor damage limited to a few blocks along east 32nd Street. Some people had grown accustomed to going out and looking as the alarms sound. Others paid no attention at all.

Allen spent about 15 minutes at St. John's Hospital trying to assess, and then made his way over to Joplin Health Care facility just east, where he came across an ambulance crew. When he asked them if there was a staging area where he could get set up with the dogs and gear, the crew told him he could probably set up anywhere and be able to help. Wherever Allen ended up, his help would be greatly needed. One of his crew members had ended up at The GreenBriar elderly care facility at 26th Street and Moffett Avenue where there was reportedly a total collapse. It would be a miracle if there were any survivors.

Allen drove down 32nd Street to Range Line Road, then

north to get to the parking lot of The Home Depot Store where emergency workers and volunteers were pulling people from the wreckage. The area looked as bad as any warzone. The couple pulled their pickup truck and trailer onto the parking lot of the Aldi grocery store across the street. Before they could even get out of the parking lot, the cadaver dogs had already targeted locations in the rubble. He was reminded again that it would truly be a miracle if the storm had left less than 1,000 casualties.

When Allen reached the parking lot of The Home Depot store, there was only one ambulance crew there, but many fire trucks. Everybody was working independently to free people from the fallen building. There were many people on the parking lot that had been drawn to the flashing emergency lights of the rescue vehicles parked among the massive piles of debris. Allen treated one man, performing a needle chest decompression under near-battlefield conditions. He would have to improvise and do the best that he could with whatever materials were readily available. Allen said, "There was very little about the conditions and environment that would be considered sterile by any standards," but he had to perform the necessary emergency procedure, right then and there. He would try to rub off what he could with a dirty shirt sleeve and use an alcohol wipe swab that someone had given him. After the procedure was completed, Allen transferred the man to the next ambulance that arrived on the scene and then went back into search and rescue mode.

Initially, Alicia and her work dog, "Unsinkable Molly Brown," went to the outside of the fallen back wall of Wal-Mart. "Molly", a 9-year-old chocolate lab, was able to distinguish both live and dead human scent. Molly is truly an "unsinkable" dog, according to Allen. She was the only search and rescue dog in the world at that time with a pacemaker of her own.

Alicia was working behind the fallen back walls of the Wal-Mart Store within the first 30 minutes of the storm's impact. Molly immediately signaled to Alicia that there was a live person or persons in an area behind the wall. When Alicia tried to get some of the men to remove pieces of the broken wall so Molly could get further into the debris, some of the men insisted on getting a backhoe and pulling down large sections of the wall. With 20 years of disaster search and rescue experience behind her, Alicia knew there were times to push a wall down and times to not. She believed this was one of those times that you definitely should not. Doing so could possibly cause the wrong results and end up burying the person or persons under the rubble. Unable to assist further at that time, she pulled the dog away from the collapsed wall and walked over to see if she could help out at the damaged Academy store about 2 blocks west. When Alicia and Molly arrived at the front of the Academy, they were turned away because of looters who were breaking in to steal unlocked firearms inside the store. Police locked the building down to prevent anyone from going in or out until they could get more law enforcement on site to secure the weapons. Alicia returned to the Wal-Mart to have Molly work inside the store.

Sometime after the events of that day, Allen had the opportunity to speak with a Christian believing journalist. This journalist asked Allen what kind of faith he was seeing. He had to ask the questions three times before it would sink in with Allen what he was asking. They were standing near 25th Street and Kentucky Avenue.

Allen answered, "Look around. Look at all this. There are less than 100 people who have lost their lives as of yet. People are already starting to tear things down so they can begin their process of rebuilding. If you are looking at all this and are unable to see or even think that there is something here that is stronger than all of us, that played such a huge role, then you are looking through someone else's eyes. You can't look around at all of this and come to any other conclusion."

Days later, when the final fatality number was announced at 161, Allen was convinced there was a much higher power at work. When you consider the amount of damage, the incredible footprint, and number of people affected, for there not to have been more casualties, there had to be a higher power working. Allen said, "There had to be a huge hand of protection over the people for those actual numbers not to be anywhere near the initial expected assessment." God was certainly busy that day.

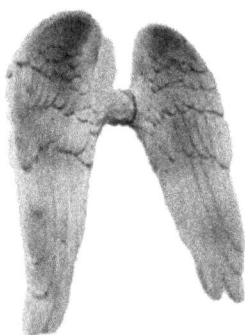

CHAPTER 11
WHAT I WITNESSED

My wife, Rosie, son, Dalton, and I were home on that Sunday afternoon. We were aware of the tornado watches and warnings coming into the area. These weather advisories were frequent in the Midwest that time of year. Many came and went over the years. Occasionally, some storms resulted in damage and destruction in the surrounding areas, with limited numbers of injuries or deaths.

About 5:15, Sunday afternoon, I left home in Silver Creek, Missouri, southeast of Joplin, Missouri, and headed to church on the northwest side of Joplin. As soon as I got on I-44, I could see the intense dark cloud from the storm as it approached southwest Joplin several miles ahead. Rosie called and said that a tornado was on the ground and headed into town. Because of the cables dividing the highway, I could not turn around. I would have to drive 2 miles towards the storm to the next exit on Main Street to get back home. Then the rain started. I made it to the Main Street exit and started back east. Immediately the rain intensified. As the visibility dropped to almost nothing, I was fortunate there were no other cars in my lane back to Range Line Road. It was like driving in a swimming pool. As soon as I pulled onto the next exit off-ramp, the rain stopped. There were low black clouds blowing to the east at ground level. It reminded me of smoke from burning tires blowing in the wind. I made it home and huddled in the basement with Rosie and Dalton. Thirty minutes later, as the storm was leaving the city on the east side, we could hear the "freight train" roar and rumble as the tornado was churning through Duquesne, Missouri about 3 miles away.

With no cell service, Dalton and I drove to check on my parents and Rosie's mother. Without any means of communication, we had no idea what to expect. My parents lived in south-central Joplin and were spared any damage. Rosie's mother lived in the Sunset Ridge area on the southwest area of Joplin. To get to her house, we had to take many detours driving far south of Joplin and come back from the west. We were able to get close enough where we could walk to her house and found that she and her husband were alright, with only moderate damage to their home. By now, nightfall had arrived, interrupted by scattered light from emergency vehicles. Homes only a block or two from hers were totally destroyed in the direct path.

We were able to weave our way back towards my office at 20th Street in Joplin. We were following a rescue vehicle down unrecognizable side streets, over sections of chain link fences, tree branches, and unimaginable, unidentifiable debris. The landscape gave no clues as to where we were, with absolute destruction everywhere. When we drove 4 to 5 blocks, we finally recognized the striping on 20th Street, but still were not sure of our exact location. We walked several blocks and found that our main office building was intact with only broken windows. Our secondary record storage building to the north had the roof flipped over onto the parking lot, but it broke the force of the direct wind. The center of the storm had passed just 2 to 3 blocks away. There were 7 buildings on that block that eventually were taken down due to the winds or the damage.

Over the next few weeks, we were able to treat some patients using another doctor's undamaged facility. There were several occasions where patients would call with sawdust, or a debris, foreign body, or corneal abrasion that needed to be addressed. On those occasions, I called the police department to get permission to drive through the curfew zone to get to the office. It was so eerie to go across once busy intersections at night and see nothing but debris piles highlighted by National Guard emergency lighting. It was dead silent. Without electricity restored yet, those procedures were performed with the patient often having to hold the flashlight as I worked.

As I look back, had Rosie not been able to reach me, or had I not turned back after she called, the timing and my route on the way to church would have placed me very close to the direct path of the storm at the exact time it crossed Schifferdecker Avenue.

CHAPTER 12
RIGHT PLACE AT THE RIGHT TIME

"The angel of the LORD encamps around those who fear Him, and rescues them."—**Psalm 34:7 (NASB)**

S teve was sitting in his living room on May 22, 2011, in his home near Main Street in Joplin, Missouri. He was spending a leisurely Sunday afternoon watching television. He heard the storm warning sirens sound but did not take much notice. He remembered so many times before when the sirens sounded... and nothing ever happened. Steve had no reason to expect anything different on this hot, sunny afternoon. He had his storm warning radio on but had turned it off some time earlier despite numerous watches or warnings in Kansas. The number of announcements for an area some distance away from his house became annoying to him, so he just turned the radio off. By the time the watches and warning announcements had shifted to include Joplin, Steve had long since silenced the radio. He would never hear the report of the impending storm.

Steve was well aware that there was a storm warning somewhere in the area, but the thought of it actually hitting Joplin never crossed his mind. He had no idea there was a tornado on the ground headed directly for his house. Even as his ears began popping from the low air pressure associated with the storm, Steve had not yet considered a tornado a possibility. He still thought this was just a bad storm.

As Steve sat in his living room recliner, he looked west through the dining room window toward St. John's Hospital and could see the black sky. Even the near pitch-black darkness outside did not give him much reason for alarm. Still, he decided it might be a good idea to head to the safety of his bedroom closet just in case. He had no idea that the tornado was on the ground only a few blocks away, chewing up everything in its path.

Steve had bronchitis and was taking two different inhalers to assist in his breathing. On his way through the dining room, he grabbed the inhalers from the table and put one in each pocket of his sweatpants as he moved back through the living room on his way to the bedroom closet. He reasoned that the amount of clothes in the closet would give him more than enough protection if it was needed. If by chance the ceiling did come down, he would be in a pile of clothes on the closet floor. The walk-in closet was very near to the center of the house. It was in the southwest corner of the bedroom that was on the northeast corner of the house. The house, built in the 1925, was constructed with lathe and plaster in the 9-foot-high walls, and had solid wooden doors.

When he got into the bedroom, he saw a white plastic patio chair sitting in the corner behind the half-open bedroom door. On that chair was his spare pillow from the bed. With the bedroom door all the way opened, it would leave a small triangular area between the back of the door and the two corner walls. The chair sat in the very corner behind the door.

When Steve got into his bedroom, he felt like he was supposed to be sitting in that $30 plastic lawn chair. Steve said, "It was as if something told me to sit on that chair behind the door and hold the pillow over my head." He would go on to say that "that something" was "the Good Lord" who was directing him into that corner. Rather than go the extra 2 feet into the clothes closet, Steve sat down on the plastic chair, placed the spare pillow over his head, and pulled the door open toward his chest. He would hold on to the glass doorknob as tight as he could. The door and two corner walls formed a small triangle, creating the refuge where Steve weathered the storm. Almost instantly as he sat down in the chair everything started breaking loose.

When the first blast of debris-filled wind hit the house, Steve realized that this was more than just a bad storm. It was actually a tornado. Steve later said that he will never forget the sound that the pummeling winds made as they devoured the house around him. He compares the sound of the storm to the loud crunching, grinding, and breaking of ice cubes from the biggest ice crusher you could imagine.

The roof of the house did not last long as the winds, coming out of the south to southwest, splintered it and took it away. With the support and the protection of the roof gone, the outside walls of the house quickly ripped apart. Steve could feel the pounding winds push and pull the two corner walls behind his chair, but they withstood the fury of the wind. The walls in the corner to his back felt like they were breathing as they flexed against the wind. The wind was pulling at the door, trying to yank the knob from his grasp. The door and walls behind him would help shield him from a large amount of the debris, but Steve still got peppered by tiny wood chips and asphalt as the winds drove them into everything in their path.

Without any protection from the rain and debris directly overhead, Steve knew that he went through the eye of the storm, but doesn't remember much of a lull or break in the pounding from the wind and debris. As he sat behind the door, he was pummeled by flying debris and driving rain for about 10 minutes. He prayed to God to "make the storm stop." He could not open his eyes due to the mass of debris in the air. He could feel the suction of the wind swirling around him as he sat behind the door on the lightweight plastic chair. He was doing everything he could to be able to hang on to the doorknob until the wind finally died down.

After the wind, pounding hail, and pouring rain stopped, Steve was able to push some of the debris deposited at his feet away and stand up. He would spend the next several minutes digging insulation and storm slurry debris out of his nose, ears, mouth, and eyes. There was a rescue worker who arrived very quickly after the storm to help Steve get out of the rubble that surrounded his former home.

Once he had cleared more of the debris from his eyes, he could look in any direction from his front yard and see that no structure for several blocks was left standing. The roof of his house was completely torn off. Nearly all of the outside walls of the house were missing. The only walls inside the house that were left standing were the walls in that corner where he sat on that lightweight plastic lawn chair and the closet to his left. The surviving, standing walls only stretched about 6 feet in both directions from that corner where Steve sat. The rest of the house was essentially missing. The garage was gone, leaving not much more than a memory of its previous existence. Even the concrete slab of the garage floor was nowhere to be found.

Had Steve chosen to find safety in his closet, he most likely would have survived the destructive wind damage, but he would have had to climb up over the closet walls to get out of the debris-barricaded door.

Getting his bearings, Steve decided to head toward Main Street, about a block away, for medical assistance from some of the rescue workers who were beginning to show up in the vicinity. It took him almost 20 minutes to get over and through the debris in his path to travel less than a block. As he walked past Arby's restaurant, he noticed that about all that was left of that business was the tile floor and a steel beam arch overhead.

Steve muses that he has been on a motorcycle at 140 miles per hour, in a car at 160 miles per hour, and now he has been in a white plastic lawn chair in winds of over 200 miles per hour.

Steve says that the only rationale for deliverance through the storm and for his survival is the "guardian angel" who watched over him that day. He knows of no logical reason why he made it through the storm in one piece. He said that "it must be that the Good Lord has something planned for me."

◆ ◆ ◆

Judy was spending Sunday afternoon with her parents at their home east of Missouri Southern State University when she heard about the severe storm warnings in the Joplin area. She decided to head back across town to her own house just west of St. John's Hospital before the weather conditions worsened. Before she left, she called her daughter, Linda, who had been in Columbia, Missouri visiting family members. Linda, her daughter, Keyarah, and Linda's sister, Patty, all resided together with Judy. Linda and Patty had already left Columbia and were about 40 miles from home.

Judy had planned to stop at Dillon's Grocery Store on 20th Street to pick up some groceries. As she left her parent's house, she noticed the sky was mostly clear. Driving west on 7th Street into town, she saw some darker clouds off to the southwest, but nothing that seemed out of the ordinary. When she reached the intersection of 7th Street and Range Line Road, the storm warning sirens sounded. Judy called Michael, her employer, to report that the sirens were sounding, even though the sky was still mostly clear. Michael's wife, Kathy, at their home several miles south and west of the city limits, said the sky was clear at their home too. They had no idea that a colossal storm was developing on the west side of the city.

Judy continued driving south on Range Line Road and turned west on 20th Street. The sky had begun to get a bit darker, but it still did not seem to be anything unusual for a typical springtime storm in Joplin. By the time she reached Dillon's Grocery Store, the storm warning sirens had stopped. She noticed that the air seemed different as she got of her parked car and the sky was considerably darker.

Shortly after Judy reached the checkout line with her items, the storm warning sirens began to sound again. Jaz and John, the store managers, began to escort everyone to the produce coolers on the west end of the store. The cashier had just finished ringing up Judy's grocery sale and asked her to head back to the cooler to join the other customers already there. The new cashier then turned and ran to join the others. Judy assured both Jaz and John, as well as Nicole, the cage clerk, that she would be able to make it home alright and headed toward the front door.

As she exited the store, the wind had picked up considerably, the storm warning sirens still blaring loudly. Nicole, a friend of Judy's for many years, grabbed the two bags of groceries and helped Judy get them to her car, still asking Judy to reconsider and come back inside to the safety of the cooler. The wind was blowing strongly from the south, but the rain had not started yet. Judy reassured Nicole that "God is going to take care of us" and gave her a hug. Judy told Nicole to just go back into the store, get into the cooler, and pray. Nicole then turned and ran back inside the safety of the store. Judy had no idea that the front wall of the storm was headed directly for her and was only about 8 blocks away.

Getting situated in her car and tightening her seat belt, Judy noticed a full-size SUV pull into the parking spot just to the left of her Buick Century. As the storm warning sirens continued to sound, a man and a woman got out and started to run to the front door of the grocery store. Judy watched as the strong, gusting winds would pick the woman up slightly and push her along.

At that time, Judy began to wonder if maybe she had made the wrong decision by going to her car, instead of retreating to the safety of the cooler inside the store. She tried to open her car door but was unable. The car door had already suctioned shut. Judy quickly realized that she was in big trouble. When she looked to the west from the front seat of her car, she could see an enormous cloud approaching Joplin High School about 6 blocks away. The wind had picked up tremendously, and the rain was coming down in sheets.

Suddenly, her cell phone rang. It was Norman, a friend who worked with the Webb City Fire Department. Thinking she was at home, he warned her to take cover as the storm was probably right on top of her, and then he hung up. He did not hear Judy screaming to him that she was not at home, as he probably thought, but was stranded in front of Dillon's Grocery Store. Judy called the fire station back and Mark, the captain, told her that they were taking cover from the approaching storm at the Webb City Fire Station. Mark could not hear her and hung up before Judy could let him know to tell Norman where she was stranded. The sky had by now turned nearly pitch black. Almost instantly, the wind grew even stronger.

Judy put her cell phone in the palm of her hand and grabbed the steering wheel tightly. She pressed her feet down on the brake pedal and braced herself. As she looked toward the storm, now bearing down on her from the west, she watched as the churches and houses just 2 blocks away began to disintegrate and fly into the darkness that surrounded her. As the car started rocking violently back and forth, all Judy could do was scream out and pray.

Judy screamed and begged for God to protect her family who were heading home on I-44. She begged for God to protect her parents, her family, her friends, the patients in their office, and the people of Joplin. She begged for God to let her live to see her grandson who was to be born in January. With a loud crash, all the windows of Judy's car shattered from the debris and disappeared into the loud blackness. Judy did a lot of screaming, confessing, and praying as the storm raged on around her.

All of a sudden, the rear end of the large SUV that had been parked next to her car was lifted off the ground by the incredible force of the wind and moved over on top of the driver's side of Judy's car. The noise was deafening. It was like nothing she had ever heard before. The concrete block front wall and part of the roof of Dillon's Grocery Store then collapsed onto Judy's car. The front and roof of the car were smashed by the falling concrete blocks, rocks, and lumber. Judy was getting pounded by massive amounts of debris from every direction. There were concrete blocks that were flying into the debris-filled interior of Judy's car through the back window. The back window of the car, like all the other open windows, acted as a funnel for the flying debris. As those moments went on, the interior of the car was soon filled to Judy's shoulder level with the debris. There was a large board with a metal rod on the end that flew through the back of the car, stopping just short of going through Judy's seat.

After the pounding from the blocks, rocks, and boards that bombarded Judy, she was drenched with freezing-cold rain. When the rain stopped, she was pounded by softball-sized hailstones for another couple of minutes. It seemed to Judy that it would never end.

When the storm had finally passed, Judy was stuck in a pile of debris inside her car, and she had several large cuts on her forehead. She was able to call Linda on her cell phone that was still clutched in her hand. There were two men who arrived to help dig Judy out of her wrecked, debris-filled front seat. A Joplin police officer was there on the scene very shortly to help the injured. After the men dug Judy out of the ravaged car, the police officer told her that he saw no way that she should have survived the storm. Seeing the massive mound of debris that filled the front seat of Judy's car, he said there was nowhere else she could have been inside the car and survive. If she was just 1 foot in any direction, the outcome would have been different.

The officer told Judy that he would get an ambulance to the store as quickly as he could to get her to the hospital, but she told him she worked for a doctor and would get checked out in the office. She just wanted to go home. When the police officer asked Judy where the doctor's office and her home were, he just shook his head and they both cried as he told her that she did not have a home or a place of employment. Both of those buildings were destroyed in the storm.

The emergency and rescue workers turned their attention toward the people who sought shelter in the produce cooler inside the store. Becky and her daughter, Maggie, had parked their car very close to where Judy's car was on the parking lot just moments before the storm smashed into the store. These two women rode out the storm in the produce cooler with 17 other people, including one woman who was in her 7th month of pregnancy. The walls of the fruit and produce cooler were being slowly crushed by the force of the storm. The ceiling, measuring about 10 by 20-foot, started to arch upwards as the walls began to compress downward and in as the force of the storm continued. The cooler had been significantly compressed, but it turned out to be very survivable on this day. The rescue workers grabbed car jacks from the wrecked cars and used them to pry and lift the cooler walls to free those inside. They all escaped with only minor injuries.

Judy said that she was spared that day only by the unmerited mercy and grace of God. She believes the weight of the SUV on the top of her car, and the weight of the walls and roof of the store, kept her vehicle from being lifted up and out by the storm. Judy found out later that Linda, Patty, and Keyarah had stopped in Sarcoxie, Missouri on their way home for a bathroom break. Linda reminded Judy that they usually never make a rest stop when they are that close to home, only about 20 minutes away. That day was different though. They decided that they would have no choice but to stop, so they pulled off the interstate for about 15 minutes. Judy believes that, had the girls continued on their trip home from Springfield, Missouri without that rest stop delay, they would have been home or close to it at a very dangerous time. The effect of the storm on her life was a wake-up call for Judy. She feels stronger in some ways as compared to before that Sunday in May. She now recognizes the importance of order in her family. She realizes the frailty of things around her; specifically, life.

◆ ◆ ◆

H azel was at her home east of Connecticut Avenue in Joplin, sitting at her kitchen table, working a jigsaw puzzle, while listening to the I-70 Series baseball game. Partway through her puzzle, Hazel got a call from Sally, her next-door neighbor, who informed her that a storm was headed for Joplin and suggested that Hazel would be safer in Sally's home. Very shortly after she received that phone call, Hazel's son, Rick, also called. He told her to hang up right away and go immediately to Sally's house. Hazel still had no idea that there was a huge storm, now only about a mile away, and headed directly for her neighborhood.

Sally had an additional room built behind her home that stepped down about 3 to 4 feet below the main level of her home. She had the builders excavate the area of the yard for the room so the floor level of that additional room ended up being a couple of feet below the level of the ground outside. Sally had this room added on the east side of the back of her house to accommodate her in–home dog-grooming business. There was a small seating area with a few chairs in the middle of the 15 by 25-foot addition, where the patrons could sit while they waited for Sally to finish grooming. There was also a restroom with a walk-in shower up against the original foundation structure of the house, and a laundry area with a washing machine and a dryer located adjacent to the restroom.

As Hazel walked the 50 feet or so to Sally's front door, she had no idea that the storm was only about 3 blocks west of the house. Hazel was not paying that much attention to things around her. At the rate the storm was traveling, it would be upon her in seconds. The storm warning sirens were already silent, out of commission due to the loss of power caused by the storm. Hazel entered Sally's house through the front door and they both went through the front room and toward the kitchen to reach the steps down into the grooming area. They were almost through the kitchen and on their way down the steps when the first blast of wind from the storm struck the front of the house. The first bombardment of debris landed on the floor just behind them as they hurried together through the darkened kitchen. Racing down the stairs, they had just enough time to reach the pair of chairs in the center of the sunken room. They got to the chairs with not much more than a second to spare. There was no extra time.

Sally took out her Bible and opened it up. Both of the women placed their hands onto the opened pages together and prayed, "Lord, You are all we have!" They could not remember speaking to or communicating with each other and said nothing else until after the storm had passed.

As the women sat in those two chairs in the middle of the darkened room, Hazel recalls that the noise from the storm, now directly overhead, was incredibly and horribly loud. The noise was so overpowering that she couldn't think. She couldn't move. She couldn't do anything. While the storm was raging on all around them, Hazel remembers the sense of a hand upon her shoulder that she would describe as "God's Hand." She defines it as very soothing, with a warming peace that gave her immediate relief from the drenching rain they had just gone through.

That sense of soothing peace stayed with Hazel for just a few seconds. She could also see a vision of her grandmother sitting on the foundation of the destroyed house just above eye level from their spot in the lower room. There was also a man, whom Hazel did not recognize, standing next to and slightly behind the image of her grandmother. He was standing in clean, dry, white clothes. She described their expressions as peaceful looking. Both of them remained visible to Hazel for just a moment or two before disappearing from her sight. The peace accompanied by their presence remained with her throughout the storm.

Hazel doesn't recall seeing much debris in the air as she had her eyes closed for most of the time the storm roared overhead. There was a large amount of debris that filled much of the room, but there was very little that had ended up around the chairs where the two women sat. There was a clear, 7-foot wide, debris-free zone around them.

The massive hail pounded down on everything after the ceiling over their heads had torn away. Most of the roof of the sunken room had been torn away. Nearly Sally's entire house on the level just 3 feet above was completely gone. The strong smell of natural gas lingered in the lower level.

Almost immediately after the storm had passed, Hazel raised her arms over her head to catch a piece of sheetrock that had come loose. She held it back up against the wall to keep it from pulling completely away. As she was holding the sheetrock, Sally asked for some assistance. Hazel declined for just a moment and stared at Sally in astonishment. A Christmas wreath was hanging around Sally's neck. It had previously been hanging on a wall in Sally's bedroom near the front of the house. It had traveled the entire length of the house as the building had disintegrated around them; past the area where the kitchen had stood just seconds before, and down the back stairway to eventually land around Sally's neck. Hazel worked to hold up the falling sheetrock and free Sally from the wayward wreath around her neck. They both laughed.

Right after the storm had passed, the rain began to pick up. Sally and Hazel, unable to get past the debris blocking the stairs, made their way from the chairs to the restroom adjacent to the original foundation of the house on the west side of the room. Like the debris-free zone around the chairs, there was no debris to be found in the restroom.

Sally had a small bruise on her arm and Hazel had a cut across her arm from the storm. Neither knew how the injuries occurred. The two women sat in the restroom until Hazel's granddaughter, Melissa, stopped by Hazel's house next door to check on her grandmother. Melissa had been at the mall when the storm struck and it took her about 30 minutes to navigate the debris-filled streets to get to Hazel's house. She was looking through what was left of Hazel's house, which was essentially nothing and was unaware that her grandmother was actually safe about 50 feet to the south. Hazel and Sally tried to yell to get Melissa's attention, but it took several minutes before Melissa finally heard the two women. Melissa had two men help her pull the debris out of the stairway so Hazel and Sally could finally get out of the room. She, too, could smell the pungent odor of natural gas filling the room.

It was a week before Hazel went back to her own property. All that was left were the hardwood floors. They were picked clean of walls, furniture, and debris—no wall was left standing. Hazel worried about the deed to the house, insurance papers, and other important documents she kept in two file boxes in a closet in the back bedroom. She was also concerned about her medications which she kept in a small child's lunch box. Before Hazel arrived, her grandsons visited the site the morning after the storm to assess the damage and take photographs for Hazel. They found the two file boxes and the lunch box. All three were stacked neatly together on the bare hardwood floor near where Hazel's recliner had sat in the front living room. The recliner did not fare so well. It lay twisted and broken in the front yard.

Had Hazel not gotten the call from Sally to come next door to ride out the storm and the urgent reminder from her son, Rick, to do as Sally asked, the results at the end of that Sunday would most likely have been tragically different. The only places that would have offered enough protection were the chairs in the sunken room where they sat during the storm or the restroom where they finally ended up.

Hazel knows in her heart that there are more plans for her life. There was a distinct reason that she made it through the storm. She recognizes the feeling of the Hand of God on her shoulder that day. She was protected. She says God's angels were all around her that day.

CHAPTER 13
POWER AND PRESENCE OF GOD

"He taught me and said to me, 'Daniel, I have come to give you wisdom and to help you understand. When you first started praying, an answer was given, and I came to tell you, because God loves you very much. So think about the message and understand the vision.'"—**Daniel 9:22-23 (NCV)**

"Then an angel from heaven appeared to him to strengthen him."—**Luke 22:43 (NCV)**

On that Sunday afternoon, Geoff was in Baxter Springs, Kansas, coaching a 14-year-old-and-under girls' softball team. They had practice that afternoon from 3 p.m. to 6 p.m. Just a little bit before 5 p.m., one of the girls' mothers told Geoff that tornado warnings were in effect all over the area. Geoff, at first, couldn't believe it because the sky was beautiful and seemed perfectly clear. He gave the girls a break and went over to the dugout to grab his phone and check the weather radar and forecast. As he was looking at the radar map, he began to notice the sky was quickly starting to change. He ended practice and told the parents to take their girls home.

With what Geoff had seen on the weather radar, he got into his car and decided to head over to his parents' house near South Main Street in Joplin, Missouri. They had a basement, and he could seek protection from any rapidly developing storm. He would normally take 12th Street east out of Baxter Springs to Highway 400, then drive south to Interstate 44 east and exit onto North Main Street. This day seemed no different than any other. When Geoff turned the radio on in his car, he heard of a funnel cloud reported in Riverton, Kansas, moving toward Joplin at about 20 miles per hour. By the time he reached 12th Street and Military Road in Baxter Springs, the weather broadcaster was advising of a funnel cloud on Interstate 44. Geoff did not hear of the highway mile-marker location. He thought it would be better to drive on through Riverton about 5 miles to the north, where he hoped to end up behind that funnel and could follow it safely to the east. Aware that a funnel cloud does not often backtrack, he believed he would probably be safer behind than in front of it. Geoff would not find out until later that there were two different funnel-producing storm cells that would eventually merge together.

About the time he approached the roundabout on Highways 400 and 66 in Riverton, Kansas, Geoff drove into an incredible hailstorm. He had a hard time seeing the road ahead of him. The hailstorm lightened by the time he made it through Riverton, and he headed east into Galena, Kansas on Highway 66. When he reached Galena a few minutes later, he was met with another powerful hailstorm. This storm lasted for another minute or two before it eased. He believed he was still driving behind the funnel-producing storm cell. He continued east to Joplin. He was constantly checking the sky, mainly toward Interstate 44 to the south, for any rapid changes in the weather. He could not see anything unusual in the sky toward the south. He figured he would take Schifferdecker Avenue south then head east on 32nd Street to get to his parents' home. He drove past the storm spotter who was watching the sky from the location near Carousel Park, a few blocks west of Schifferdecker Avenue, on 7th Street. Geoff then turned south on Schifferdecker Avenue, not realizing the huge storm that had been tracked from Interstate 44 was now bearing down on the Sunset Ridge subdivision located near 30th Street and Schifferdecker Avenue. He was headed directly into its path.

A couple of minutes later, storm chaser Jeff Piotrowski pulled up to that same storm spotter at Carousel Park to tell them that the city needed to activate the storm warning sirens immediately as there was a huge funnel that had formed due south of their location, near 32nd Street.

As he approached the stoplight at the 26th Street intersection, Geoff watched as a large piece of either metal or wood flew through the air from the west and struck the cab of a pickup truck about four lengths in front of his Chevrolet Impala. Geoff watched in astonishment as the truck slowed down, drifting to the left, and stopping next to the curb at the corner of 26th Street. It was taking him a moment to process what was developing around him. He turned the radio off to help him concentrate. The sky had become nearly black. The rain and the hail began to come down in torrents.

Geoff felt a lurch as his Impala was lifted straight up from the ground by the strong force of the winds—all the windows blew in as the car was lifted several feet off the ground. The powerful winds that lifted the car turned it 180 degrees back toward the north and gently set it down on the road. He realized he was right in the middle of a tornado. Geoff had survived many adverse situations during his years in law enforcement. He had been shot once, stabbed twice, run over by a drunk driver, and survived. He had survived 25 surgeries and survived brain cancer. Now he had done something incredibly stupid by driving his car into the center of a tornado. He felt like such an idiot. Geoff believed this would be something he would not survive. Even his history of storm spotting experience was of no help now.

As Geoff watched things unfold before his eyes, he tried to reason how to get out of the situation quickly. He cinched down his seatbelt, reasoning if somebody was going to find the car, it would be easier to identify him if he was still in it. Geoff realized this was definitely not a good place to be.

He knew the southwest-northeast orientation of Interstate 44 was generally parallel to the common path of the storms that traveled through Joplin. The history of past storms in the Joplin area showed tracks that usually stayed on one side of Interstate 44 or the other. A storm to the south usually stayed south. A storm to the north usually stayed north. Geoff was on the north side of the Interstate. The tornado was on the north side of the Interstate. He reasoned he needed to get to the south side as quickly as possible to be safe. He had no idea of the size and strength of the storm that was now 5 or 6 blocks away.

Geoff turned his car around to get as far south as fast as he could. He noticed the row of pear trees that lined the northwest corner of 26th Street and Schifferdecker Avenue were almost all laying flat to the ground, getting beaten by the violent wind coming from the northwest. As soon as he got his car facing south, before he even got out of the intersection on 26th Street, a large, full-size suburban literally fell out of the sky and landed upside down just in front of him.

Geoff's car started to pull sideways as he drove south on Schifferdecker Avenue. The rain was pouring in sheets as he tried to keep control of the car in the crosswinds. He does not remember much noise as all his concentration was on just getting out of the neighborhood in one piece. He dodged telephone poles and wires and all sorts of debris, large and small. He knew this was not a place where he needed to be and decided he was just going to have to blast on through to get out of the middle of the chaos as quickly as he could. He could see the houses on both sides of the street begin to implode. There would be times that he could see a block away, followed immediately by visibility that would drop down to 30 feet or so. He caught glimpses of roofs being peeled back from the houses in the neighborhood near the ponds on the east side of Schifferdecker Avenue. He had to speed past and dodge debris flying across the road in front of him, including fences, telephone poles, tree branches, and all sorts of shredded building remnants. As he got closer to 32nd Street, he saw the houses on the west side of the road, in Sunset Ridge, begin to disintegrate. He saw the neighborhoods on both sides of him were literally blowing away.

As Geoff sped toward 32nd Street, he watched as those houses to the west down 32nd Street were flying apart also. He wasted no time in getting as far away from that corner as he possibly could. By the time he got to about 40th Street and Schifferdecker Avenue, Geoff realized he had made it through in one piece. As he got to Main Street on Interstate 44, he came up on many cars that were crowded under the overpass to avoid the hail that was still falling. He decided to drive on to his parent's house as he was only about 10 blocks away.

When he looked at his car after he pulled into the carport at his parents' house, Geoff noticed there was a huge indentation in the roof of the vehicle. It looked just like a huge 4 by 4-foot handprint. There were only minimal scratches on the side of the car. The indentation on the roof was pushed down about 8 to 10 inches. Geoff believes something that would have made such a large, deep dent in the whole roof of the car would have made some type of noise or moved or jolted the car as it happened, but Geoff says there was nothing he was aware of to cause the dent. Geoff has no logical explanation for the dent and doesn't claim to know what God has planned for him, but he is aware that he was miraculously spared. He felt God had to be present that day for reasons that he does not understand.

Geoff would later talk with one of his friends who worked on weather models for NASA. His friend told him, "When you get close to a tornado with two funnels that are combining or merging, there is a dead zone of about 30 to 40 yards between the two funnels. The winds will do some very strange things in that zone. The wind speeds are still high, around 100 miles per hour or so, but nothing like the winds in the vortex of 200 plus miles per hour." There were two funnel-producing storm cells that merged into one on that day. The first storm cell tracked was coming straight from the west into Joplin. It was the storm cell that Geoff drove through while going through Riverton and Galena. The other storm cell was being tracked up Interstate 44 from the southwest. The piece of debris that struck the truck in front of him on Schifferdecker Avenue came out of the west. The pear trees were laying down in the winds coming out of the north. The rotation from the funnel that came through Sunset Ridge would have produced winds at that intersection out of the south or southeast, not the north or west. The two funnels were heading toward each other from both sides of where Geoff sat in his car. Geoff believes that, had he been 100 feet in any direction from where he actually was, the results would have been drastically different.

◆ ◆ ◆

David was sitting in his living room watching a televised weather report that Sunday afternoon in his home near St. John's Hospital, in Joplin, Missouri. The first storm warning sounded about 10 to 15 minutes earlier. David, like most other people, heard the sirens but did not give them much credence. The people of Joplin had grown accustomed to hearing warnings for storms that rarely resulted in damage. David became a little more aware of the darkening sky after hearing the first siren, but he felt no sense of urgency. He became a little more interested when he heard the second siren sound. He considered for just a moment about doing what he would normally do when the sirens sounded during storms in the past—sit in his chair and watch the weather reports. He had no idea that the storm was headed directly toward him. Today, David felt something different in his spirit. He felt he should go to the sunken, eastern back room of his house—the floor level in that room was about 3 feet below the floor level of the main rooms.

Once there, David sat on the bottom steps leading down to it. David heard a noise that sounded like golf balls hitting the side of the house. He believes the sounds were more likely from debris than hail. The sky outside had turned almost pitch black as the storm approached. From where he was sitting, David could still see the television was on in the living room. It displayed a funnel cloud that was only a few blocks from his back door. Through a nearby window, he saw the tornado moving in as the shroud of rain lifted for only a moment. He covered his head with a blanket and lay down across the stairs. In just another second or two, the power went out and the house grew dark.

Almost immediately after the lights went out, the fury of the storm presented. In an instant, all the windows and exterior doors blew out of the house. David had not noticed any of the noises consistent with a tornado until it had already hit. The fact those sounds did not announce the approaching storm caught David a bit by surprise. Once the windows blew out, the noise level changed dramatically. He compares the sound to that of a jet descending on his house. It seemed to go on forever and he wondered when it would finally stop. David looked out from underneath the blanket once or twice to see the mass of debris flying through the air outside.

As the eye of the storm passed, David had a false sense of hope it was over, but it proved to be a fleeting reprieve as the back wall of the storm came in. David recalls looking out the window and seeing the blackness of the inside surface of the eye wall.

As David lay there on the stairs, praying continually, he felt the force of the wind and pressures pull his body toward an open window about 6 feet away. At the same time, he could feel a stronger force pushing him back down to the floor. This repeated several times during the storm. As soon as he felt the pressure act as if he was being lifted toward the window, a force that felt much like that of a gentle hand would push him back to the floor. The hand was strong but not harsh. The gentle force felt as if it covered his whole back.

When the winds finally stopped, David felt water dripping onto his head. He got up and started out of his house when he noticed part of the kitchen wall and roof was gone. Debris was all over the house from who knows where. Even the wallpaper border was removed by the winds from the living room walls. The rain finally stopped after about 15 minutes after the winds let up. When he finally got to the front porch and out to the street, he saw that more than three-quarters of his roof was gone. Most of the south wall of the rock house was missing. The bark on the two large trees in David's front yard had been stripped from the trunks. There was also a big tree with a large, intact root ball that had been deposited in his yard. A neighbor told him that the huge tree had originated from a yard several blocks away. He believes the tree that blew to the north side of his home brought protection from the strong southern winds from the back wall of the storm. His house was the only house within several blocks with any walls left standing.

"When the Hand of God is present; you can sense power and peace," David said. "It was present the entire time the house was being pounded by the storm."

David has felt God's presence before, but never as strongly as on May 22. Today, David has more assurance of who his God is and now feels greater urgency to get the message of the hope in Christ out to other people. He is uncertain what the future holds for him, but he is certain God truly has a plan for him. His confidence has grown considerably since the storm, and he has no problem telling others he was spared by the grace and mercy of God that day.

CHAPTER 14
GOD'S PROTECTION

"My God sent His angel and shut the lions' mouths so that they couldn't hurt me. He did this because He considered me innocent. Your Majesty, I haven't committed any crime."—**Daniel 6:22 (GW)**

"So the devil left Jesus, and angels came and took care of Him."—**Matthew 4:11 (NCV)**

Eli, 5, had just gone inside his home on West 26th Street, near Cecil Floyd Elementary School, when a tornado warning was broadcast on television. His parents, Melissa and Clay, were aware of the bad weather in the area. The weather reports tracked the main part of the storm farther north, through the Carl Junction or Airport Drive area, nearly 7 miles north of their home.

The drill that Eli's family routinely practiced with bad-weather storms was the same. Eli would gather with his sisters, Zoe, 11, Emma, 7, and his 3-year-old brother, Luke. Without a basement, their "safe place" was on the floor in a narrow hallway in the most interior part of the house. It was one step below the larger front room. Melissa would sit on the floor in the hallway with the children surrounding her. They would pull the blankets from the linen closet and huddle on the floor. Clay would typically pull the mattress off one of the beds and crouch down with his family, holding the mattress over their heads. When the tornado warning was announced, Zoe went to the hall closet and grabbed all the blankets from the linen closet and the pillows from their beds and got down on the floor with the others.

Clay had been outside scanning the sky, mainly to the north toward Carl Junction and Airport Drive area, when the storm siren first sounded. The sky to the north did not look bad. The overall weather conditions did not look that unusual. The color of the sky, the clouds, and the general look seemed normal. He dismissed that anything would really happen and stayed outside watching the sky. Melissa and the children were all still huddled together in the hallway with the blankets and pillows. It was still and calm as they sat there on the floor in the hallway praying. After the siren stopped, Clay continued scanning the sky, mainly to the north, and noticed some very low clouds wisping across the sky. They were acting differently than what he had seen just moments before.

Clay began to look toward the south. There were many large trees just west and south of his home obstructing his line of sight beyond a few blocks. The sky was still pretty bright. There were even blue patches visible. He began to hear the telltale sounds of a freight train and quickly realized it was from a tornado. Bright blue flashes reflected off the low clouds, as transformers several blocks away were exploding. He ran inside and yelled to his family, "This is it! It's happening!" Melissa yelled to Clay, "Grab the mattress! Grab the mattress!" He grabbed the mattress from the nearest bedroom and dragged it into the hallway to pull it over his family. He crouched down under with his back toward the front living room. Melissa and the children all leaned forward under the mattress. Then the lights went out. Only about 30 seconds had transpired since Clay first heard the "train" in the distance.

The noise was tremendous. Melissa was praying out loud, "God, keep my kids safe." Even with all the excitement, it was relatively peaceful, at least for a few seconds more. They could hear the loud crashing and breaking of glass, followed by more loud crashes and deafening booms as larger objects were pounding the outside of their home. Clay told himself the damage may not be extensive, and he hoped it might be limited to broken windows, siding, and maybe a tree or two down. All the while, the noise from the wind grew louder. Clay thought there was still a possibility of limited damage until suddenly all the remaining glass in the house seemed to crash at once. The narrow hallway became a wind tunnel. Clay began to lose his grip on one side of the mattress.

"On a scale of 1 to 10, the level of chaos was easily a 10," Clay would later say, "Then it got much worse."

Clay said, "In just a few seconds, it was like a bomb had gone off and the house literally exploded." The house just to the west of their home blew off its foundation and smashed into the west side of their home. That impact weakened the structural integrity of their home, destroying any hope that it would be able to offer much more protection in the storm. Melissa and the girls were screaming, and the girls were all praying. The entry door was torn off and their front room disintegrated. Clay was pushed forward, then lost his grip on the mattress. He was pulled out backwards through where the living room had stood just seconds before. Melissa and two of the three children seemed to just fall out of what was left of their hallway. The house was leveled. The subfloor was peeled up in places, revealing the concrete slab below.

Melissa was blown about 125 feet east of the couple's house, behind the destroyed duplex of their next-door neighbor. Emma and Luke were still clinging to her legs and arm. They were in the same order as they had been sitting while huddling in the hallway just moments before. Melissa still clung onto the mattress as tight as she could.

Clay ended up much farther away. He was blown 250 feet to the southeast, at times 10 to 15 feet off the ground, and finally landed in the smaller branches of a large tree as it was being blown over by the wind.

Zoe was deposited about 10 feet away from her mother, under the protection of a door wedged into the debris. The door gave her some protection from the debris and hail that would follow with the back half of the storm.

Eli was missing.

Since they were located near the northern edge of the storm wall, the duration of the calmer eye of the storm was very brief, but brought with it a blanket of luminescence. Clay could see Melissa about 100 feet away and yelled for her to stay down—the storm was not over yet. Debris from the back half of the storm pelted them. The hail was enormous and merciless. Melissa was able to get Emma, Luke, and herself under the nearby door with Zoe to get out of the hail and freezing rain. There was a lot of lightning, low to the ground for a short period of time. As quickly as he could free himself from the safety of the tree, Clay climbed to the tops of the numerous debris piles and called out for Eli. He had difficulty trying to figure out where he was. There were no recognizable landmarks to be found. He saw Melissa's car tangled in a nearby tree.

Melissa and Clay looked frantically for Eli for about 5 to 10 minutes. They walked among the debris piles searching for signs of their son, calling out his name. Zoe finally heard him answer. When they found him, he was rolled up inside a rug like a burrito; his foot sticking of from the end of the rug grabbing their attention. The rug was in a low ditch behind the next-door neighbor's house, only about 25 feet east of where the family's home once stood.

As they unrolled the rug to free him, they thought it was unusual that the rug was not a free- floating area rug that lay loosely, as in somebody's kitchen or hallway. It was a large wall-to-wall rug, big enough to cover a sizable living room floor. It was not from anywhere in their house nor did they recognize it from any of their neighbor's homes. To this day they are not sure where it came from.

They described the rug as folded over, then snugly rolled around Eli. They compared the rug to children at play rolling each other up inside towels or blankets. It was similar to the technique that a pediatrician or an emergency room doctor might use in rolling up a small child, as a papoose, to treat them.

When checking Eli over, Melissa and Clay noticed he did not have even one scratch, and had only a small bruise on one elbow. As they talked with Eli, he told them, "The man with the brown hair rolled him up inside the rug."

Zoe had a sore neck and a large knot and torn muscle in her leg where the doorknob hit her. The door that landed near her shielded her from the flying debris, sparing her from potentially worse injuries.

Clay went back the next day to get some shoes, clothes, and personal items. He walked to the location where the door had protected first Zoe, then Melissa, Emma, and Luke. Directly over that spot were remnants of the door-jamb held together by stapled electrical wire resting on a small sapling tree. Clay found a necklace with a small cross hanging on a nail directly over where Zoe was found. It did not belong to anyone in their family. The family considers the cross on the necklace as a sign of hope and remembrance that they were protected during a literal storm that forever changed their lives.

◆ ◆ ◆

On May 21st, Shannon's parents, Tim and Kathy, came over to have dinner with her, her two children, and her roommate, Pam.

While everyone was still eating, Tim stood up from the kitchen table to look around a bit. He walked over to a small hallway just off the kitchen and opened a door across the hall from the bathroom. It opened to a small closet underneath the stairway of the two-story home. He told Shannon, "This looks like this would be a real good place to go if a storm ever came." Shannon agreed and said they had thought the same thing. It seemed a little odd to Shannon that her father would make such a comment. It was just something to keep in mind if there ever was a need to seek shelter from a bad storm in the future. She had no idea she would be depending on the advice in just a day.

Shannon usually spent Sundays with her parents, visiting into the evening before heading home, but this day was different. Shannon decided to head back to her home in Joplin a few hours earlier than usual. Pam had sent her a text message to caution Shannon that storm warning sirens were sounding and asked Shannon to stay at her parents' house in Galena, Kansas. Shannon always had her phone with her but, for some reason, she never got that text. She loaded her children, Colton, 6, and Grady, 2, into her Jeep and headed for home about 6 blocks southwest of St. John's Hospital.

As she turned onto the street about a block away from her home, Shannon could hear the storm warning sirens sounding. She did not notice anything unusual in the sky as she pulled into the driveway. She decided to put both her Jeep and Pam's into the garage, just in case there was actually some bad weather and hail. By the time she made room in the garage, and she and Pam pulled both Jeeps inside, the storm warning siren had stopped.

Shannon and Pam walked outside to look at the sky to see what the sirens were about. There were tall trees preventing them from seeing the dark clouds forming just a few miles to the southwest. They did not see any cause for alarm. Shannon brought both her children into the house—Grady had fallen asleep on the ride home from her parents', so Shannon carried him in and laid him down on the couch. Then Shannon began to fold a load of laundry.

Shannon had left the windows open on the ground floor level to allow the breeze to blow through that afternoon. The storm warning sirens sounded again. She looked out the front window and, seeing nothing unusual, walked outside to check the sky.

Inside, Colton had begun to go from room to room to close the windows. Shannon went right behind Colton to open the windows back up. She did not know why she had done that, but just felt she needed to do so. The sky was getting darker to the west and southwest, but it did not look any darker than many storm clouds she had seen before. As far as she could tell, it was just another severe thunderstorm. Shannon continued to fold laundry. They had no idea that less than a mile away, things were very different.

Pam got a phone call from a co-worker who said he heard on the radio about a large tornado headed for Joplin. He told Pam it sounded like the area where their home was located. He advised them to take cover from the impending weather. As Pam was on the phone with their co-worker, Shannon was standing in the living room when the lights began to surge. They did not flicker as much as they just got much brighter and then went out.

Pam ran to the small closet that Tim had talked to them about just the afternoon before and began to make room for everybody. Shannon scooped up Grady, still asleep on the couch, and took both of the boys to the back of the closet where the ceiling sloped down to the floor. They had no idea the storm was now only about 1 to 2 blocks away from their front door. Shannon remembers looking out the window from the inside the closet and saw the trees blowing around in the yard. Pam said she was going to take another look outside when Shannon urged her to stay put in the closet with them, grabbed Pam's arm, pulled her back inside, and shut the door. Only about 20 to

30 seconds had passed since Shannon heard the second storm siren before the front wall of the storm reached their house. The door had no more than been pulled closed before a blast of wind slammed into the house. Pam held onto the doorknob the entire time as the destructive winds pummeled the house around them.

As Pam and Shannon sat there on the floor of the closet, they looked at each other with the understanding this was not just an average thunderstorm that accompanied most storm warnings. This was truly something huge. They wondered to themselves if this was really happening. It seemed surreal. The noise inside the closet intensified. When both thought it could not possibly get much louder, the noise level continued to climb to a piercing level.

Grady woke up in a confused state about halfway through the storm. Their ears all popped as the air pressure dropped, and the storm passed overhead. The air was filled with the sounds of destruction. Things were being slammed into the house. Boards in the roof and walls were crackling and snapping. It sounded like a monster was pummeling everything in the house with a baseball bat and eating it piece by piece. The increasing noise grew similar to that of a jet engine. They could feel the walls moving, much like the house was breathing in and out. Shannon was thankful for the safety of the closet and wondered if Pam would have gone outside to take that second look if she had not intervened.

Two distinctly opposite emotions surfaced in Shannon that day. She was at first in a state of total chaos and confusion. Moments later, a feeling of calming warmth covered them as they huddled in the darkened closet. She did not feel afraid of the situation. With that peace came the ability to focus on prayer. Shannon immediately began to calmly pray and thank God for keeping them safe in the storm. She thanked Him for protecting them and she thanked Him for putting His angels around them.

She thanked Him for everything. She knew they were all going to be alright. Shannon could see Colton's panic begin to subside as he called out to his Savior. He, too, was feeling the power of God that was all around them. "It felt like a warm blanket," Shannon said. Pam could feel the sense of peace as well.

While Shannon, Pam, and Colton were praying through the storm, Shannon could sense God's Hand covering the entire staircase and steadying the closet beneath it. She could see it in her mind's eye and feel it in her spirit during the storm.

The storm seemed to last forever, but Shannon knows it was probably only a few minutes until the storm had passed. Pam and Shannon could smell natural gas as they emerged from the closet and made their way to the front of the house. They were unable to get out through the front door due to the debris that had been deposited on the front porch.

Their house was still standing, but there was a significant amount of damage, and it would, as with thousands of other homes in Joplin, be unlivable after the storm. All the windows had blown out. The house was littered throughout. The south wall of the garage suffered from the direct force of the winds just south of the eye of the storm—that wall was missing. There were large parts of the roof and sections of the ceilings in different rooms that had ripped away.

When they reached the yard a few minutes after the wind and hail had subsided, the sky was still very dark and it was pouring rain. They looked around to see where they could go to get away from the rain and the gas fumes. Shannon was holding on tightly to Grady, trying to reach her family on the phone. After a short time, Shannon realized Colton was not by her side. She began to panic. There was no electricity to worry about, but there was a tremendous amount of debris with splinters of broken wood and broken glass everywhere. She searched frantically before finding him in the next-door neighbor's living room. He was kneeling in a darkened corner of the living room with his hands clasped in front of his face. He was praying.

A large doghouse that had been in Shannon's back yard for their two golden retrievers was found in the woods behind their home. They assumed, sadly, that both of their dogs had not survived the storm, as they were not anywhere to be found. There was a moment of relief and rejoicing when, shortly after, the dogs returned safely home—shaken but not injured.

Shannon says her ribs were sore for several days from holding on to the two boys as tight as she could for the duration of the storm. It was a small price to pay for the protection God provided that day.

◆ ◆ ◆

M ike and his wife, Pamela, were in town from Denver, Colorado to celebrate her mother's 80th birthday. They had attended some family functions earlier in the day at Pamela's brother's house in Carl Junction, Missouri and were enjoying the afternoon with the family when they noticed the weather starting to change. Mike, Pamela, and her mother, Mary, decided to head to Mary's house just east of Joplin High School.

Shortly after 5 p.m., as Mike was driving, he scanned the sky and thought the weather was beginning to look like it would clear up. The sun was out. It gave the impression that it was going to turn out to be a nice afternoon.

On their way to Mary's house, Pamela suggested they stop at Dillons supermarket on East 20th Street for groceries. Pamela would just run into the store quickly and get whatever she needed, and then hurry back out. Mary was sitting in the front passenger seat of her all-wheel-drive Toyota Rav 4. The sky had clouded back up a little bit; there was still some blue sky to the south and east, though to the southwest, it had begun to darken.

Soon Mike noticed how the clouds to the southwest had become dark and ugly, and it was rapidly getting worse.

As they sat in the car, the storm sirens began to sound. Mike looked around and saw nothing that resembled what he would expect with a funnel cloud. The sirens had sounded for about 3 minutes or so, but inside the store, Pamela was unaware of the sirens. Mike considered running into the store to get Pamela, but he did not want to leave Mary out in the car by herself. They would wait.

Pamela grew up in Joplin and was familiar with the development of tornadoes in the Midwest. As a native of Denver, Mike had seen some funnel clouds throughout his lifetime, but had never gone through a tornado. As Mike and Mary sat in the car waiting for Pamela to finish her grocery shopping, the sky continued to darken. Neither of them had any idea there was a large tornado on the ground less than 3 miles away, churning up anything and everything in its path as it headed directly toward them. Light rain started to fall as they patiently waited for Pamela.

Mike and Mary were growing anxious as they waited for Pamela. Soon the rain turned into a downpour and small hailstones, mixed into the rain, pelted the SUV. Despite the storm warning sirens, they believed there was nothing more to this storm than heavy rain and hail. There was no thought about the possibility of a tornado. Unknown to them, the large, very real, funnel cloud had just finished ravaging St. John's Hospital and was heading east. It was now less than 2 miles away, cutting a mile-wide swath of destruction through the city. Pamela still had not come out of the store and Mike decided to pull Mary's car up close to the storefront so Pamela would not have to walk very far.

The store manager came out to the car. He told them there was a major storm heading for them and recommended they come inside for shelter and safety. Mike told the manager they were less than a mile from Mary's house and should be able to make it there safely. Pamela emerged from the store and climbed into the backseat of the waiting car behind her mother. She was perturbed that they had closed the store and she could not buy the groceries she had gone in for. They decided to drive on to Mary's house and get the car parked under the carport for protection from the hail.

As soon as they pulled out of the parking lot onto 20th Street heading west, the downpour turned into a hailstorm. Mike managed to make it to Wisconsin Avenue, just a block west of Dillons—Mary's house was less than a mile ahead. Even though the sirens continued to sound, the thought of an actual tornado was still not considered. They just saw a deluge of rain and a big black cloud as they continued driving right into the path of the storm. The visibility in the driving rain and hail was reduced to nothing. The wall of rain prevented them from seeing any debris that may have been blowing by them. When Mike asked Pamela about the siren sounding, Pamela told of how the sirens in Joplin always seemed to give about 5 to 10 minutes of warning before the weather actually hit. By now, they only had 6 to 7 blocks to travel before they would reach Mary's house. They should have enough time to make it home safely.

The driving rain continued to intensify as they drove. The wind shifted to come at them directly from the west, blowing the rain on Mary's side of the car. By the time they had driven about 5 blocks on Wisconsin Avenue, the rain was pouring so hard Mike could not see past the front of the hood of the car. He said, "It was like trying to drive in the bottom of a swimming pool." The wipers were going as fast as they could and it was not enough to clear the windshield. He knew that there were cars probably parked on the side of the road, but he could not see them. Rather than taking a chance of hitting a parked car, Mike decided to just stop driving. He stopped in the middle of the driving lane on Wisconsin Avenue, somewhere between 24th and 26th Streets, and planned to wait out the storm there. They were unaware that the worst part of the storm was closing in on them. It was less than a half mile away.

As they waited for the rain to stop, they heard a horrible thud as something hit the front of the driver's side of the car. With the rain driving hard from the west, Mike was able to roll down the driver's window and look down to see what had blown against the car. A big black wheelbarrow had been slammed into the front left fender and was wedged under the front tire. He was beginning to think this was more than just a rainstorm. They had no idea the tornado was less than a few blocks away as Pamela told him to roll the window up.

A few moments later, there was a huge crashing sound as the windshield shattered. The car's glass sunroof shattered also. Mike rolled his driver's window down again and saw that there was a large tree or a huge branch from a very large tree lying across the front half of the car. There were leaves visible outside the windshield, both side windows, and the sunroof. The fallen tree engulfed the front half of the car. Pamela wondered out loud if it could get any worse. The rain had not stopped or let up at all. They still could not see clearly as the rain had cut their visibility to about 2 feet. Mike rolled his window up, still thinking this was just a bad rainstorm with driving winds. The rain pouring in through the sunroof created a waterfall of rain and shattered glass onto Mike and Mary in the front seats. Pamela was worried the exposed wires in the sunroof from the falling tree had caused some shorting. The bare wires were sparking as they hung down over Mike and Mary's heads. Mike turned off the ignition to reduce the sparking and crackling of the shorted-out wires. Much of the electronic instrumentation shorted out. Both Pamela and Mike say the strongest winds were taking place while the tree was sitting on top of the car.

Without warning, all the remaining windows in the car,

except the front driver's window, blew out. Pamela immediately leaned forward between the driver and front passenger seats and covered her mother with coats and jackets from the back seat. Rain and debris were still driving in from the west with an intense force. The rain continued pouring in through the broken sunroof. The wind was whistling through the broken windows. The three of them were being battered by the force of the winds and looked for anything inside the car that could be used for protection. They used a foil sunshield to try to provide Mary some protection. Mike heard Mary praying "90 miles a minute" as they continued to be pelted by the wind-driven rain and debris.

The car began to shake violently as the tornado passed directly overhead. Mike and Pamela were trying to figure a way to get out of the situation that was getting worse by the minute. They lost all concept of time as they sat there, huddled together praying. The car continued to shake, held in place by the tree. As they sat there, wondering if the wind and rain would ever cease or at least slow down, there was a loud "whoosh" and the car lurched violently to one side. There was no break in the powerful, noisy, pounding wind. They had stopped the car just far enough south on Wisconsin Avenue to miss the interior eye wall of the tornado. There was no lull in the action from start to stop. Mike rolled his window down again to see that the tree had been removed from the car. It was gone. The wheelbarrow was still stuck under the front driver's wheel. The rain began to let up a little bit and visibility improved. The wind had dropped considerably in just a matter of seconds. Pamela wanted to get out of the car immediately but was urged by Mike to stay inside.

When they finally got out of the car, Mike attempted to pull the wheelbarrow away from the car to allow him to drive the remaining 3 blocks to Mary's house. He was successful. Mike started the car and held his head out the driver's window so he could see to drive. He moved the car back and forth several times to free the vehicle of the wheelbarrow. Mike drove forward about half a block before a low hanging power line across Wisconsin Avenue, near 26th Street, halted progress. He stopped the car briefly and got out to find a new direction. When he looked around, he saw one house next to them had no roof. The next one did not have a garage left. Many of the houses he could see had major damage. Some of them were nearly annihilated. There were roofs missing on most. They quickly realized it was much more serious than they had thought. "I think we just went through a tornado," Mike said.

They were cold, covered with debris, and soaked to the bone. They needed to find some shelter somewhere because they could not get past the power line blocking Wisconsin Avenue. They decided to head back to Dillons supermarket. As they drove back in their battered, Toyota Rav 4, many people were beginning to climb out from the massive debris piles that had been their comfortable homes just minutes earlier. They were dazed and in shock. Just 2 blocks from where they rode out the storm, there were no houses to be seen. No standing structures were visible in that area. There was nothing standing between 23rd and 20th Streets. The street surface on Wisconsin Avenue looked almost as if it had been swept clean. There was very little debris that actually ended up on the surface of the road.

As Mike drove the battered car down Wisconsin Avenue back toward Dillons, people would approach the car and ask for help. Mike would welcome them into the car. Soon, nearly a dozen people were traveling in the small 5-passenger SUV; one with a broken arm, another complaining of a back injury. They all hoped to find shelter and first aid. All were in a fair degree of pain as they rode the 4 blocks to Dillons, piled atop each other in the car. Mike pulled the packed car over near 22nd Street on Wisconsin Avenue to assist a woman trapped in a car. Mike stepped out to see if he and her husband could get the woman freed from their wrecked vehicle, but was unable as she was very securely pinned inside. Knowing the woman had no injuries, Mike told the husband that they would drive over to Dillons and send somebody back to help. Mike got back into the tiny, crowded SUV and drove the remaining 3 blocks to Dillons.

When Mike pulled the over-loaded Rav 4 onto the Dillons parking lot, his heart sank. The store was destroyed. The rain was still being driven by the wind, but not to the extent that it had just a few minutes previous. There was still plenty of rain and lightning that evening. There were mangled cars lying inside the wreckage of what was left of the grocery store. The people in Mike's car asked to be taken to a hospital. Mike, being from out of town, did not know where a hospital was. Someone suggested he drive to Memorial Hall where a triage unit was set up. As they headed that direction, they were met with more downed power lines and could not proceed. One of the injured riders suggested they might be able go east on 20th Street to Connecticut Avenue, then head south to 32nd Street and on to Freeman or St. John's Hospitals. When Mike reached Connecticut Avenue, there was so much debris that travel was impossible. Because the front windshield was a shattered mess, they could not see to drive. Both Mike and Pamela would stick their heads out the side windows to navigate through the massive debris fields. They could not find a way to get out of the devastated areas.

Mike remembered the fire station on 15th Street near Connecticut Avenue. If he could reach the fire station safely, perhaps he could get his passengers some first aid. Mike looked out the window, wondering where the edge of the tornado damage might be. He knew the damage had to stop somewhere but was having no success in getting there. He could see the water tower on Range Line Road, behind Wal-Mart. He could also see green leaves on trees off in the distance. He thought that, if he could reach the trees, he would be out of the zone and could find relief and first aid there.

Mike turned east on 15th Street from Connecticut Avenue. The stoplight at the intersection was down and the power was out. There was a policeman in a yellow rain slicker directing traffic through the devastated neighborhood. When Mike asked the officer where he could take the injured people for treatment, the officer directed him to the lot where The Home Depot used to be. The officer said a triage and treatment area had been set up there. As he drove east on 15th Street, Mike saw the fire station that he had remembered previously. There was no reason to stop. It was destroyed.

As he was nearing The Home Depot, trying to get his bearings on the scope of the storm, immediately a woman approached Mike and said, "I am a nurse. I can help." The nurse and her friend took the worst of the injured from Mike's car and walked them to the triage center a few blocks away. Mike remembered seeing a long line of cars on Highview Avenue as he was headed toward Range Line Road. It might be one of the only roads open that would allow them to get back across town. There were still several people in the car—now with four flat tires—with Mike, Mary, and Pamela. Upon learning that Highview Avenue was open all the way to 7th Street to the north, they traveled to Mary's home church, Forest Park Baptist Church, for shelter or first aid treatment.

The church was open but without power, as was much of Joplin. People were milling around as they pulled into the church parking lot. Mike's passengers went inside the church to get warm. There was still some warm food left over from a college recital held earlier in the afternoon and the church members offered it to the visitors. They went to their clothing supply house to get dry clothes for the rain-soaked people. Pamela found some tablecloths to wrap around the storm victims for warmth. Just one day earlier, those tablecloths were used to cover the tables at Mary's 80th birthday party.

Mike and Pamela said there were several unexplainable miracles they witnessed or experienced on the day of the storm. When the tree landed on the car, they thought it one of the worst things that could have happened. However, that tree held their vehicle to the ground. It most likely saved their lives. Additionally, had they been just 10 seconds later, they would have been a block or two to the north and taken a direct, unprotected hit from the storm. They were exactly where they needed to be on the street in order to make it through the storm.

Mike, Pamela, and Mary came through with only minor injuries. In addition to being covered with all kinds of debris, they all had glass embedded in their heads, and had minor bruises and abrasions. Mary had a small cut on her ear. Mike had a small cut on his finger.

The family credits God for their escape from harm. They believe His Hand of protection was on them as they sat beneath the tree that guarded them from the mighty wind, keeping them grounded, and serving as a shield from many of the debris hurtling through the air.

◆ ◆ ◆

This Sunday in May was no different than any other Sunday for 10-year-old Mason. She was a 5th grader from Springfield, Missouri. She, her cousin, Lage, 14, from Neosho, Missouri, and her grandparents, Sharon and Rodney, had spent the afternoon fishing. On the way home, Rodney decided to go to The Home Depot store and pick up a few items. Neither Rodney nor Sharon saw anything unusual about the sky as they pulled into the parking lot. There were some clouds to the southwest but no rain. Rodney had gone into the store to pick up some wiring for a new garage. Sharon and the children would have gone inside with Rodney, but she spilled some water on her pants and decided to wait in the pickup truck with the grandchildren; they waited in Rodney's 1992 Ford Crew Cab, parked facing south, near the center of the parking lot. When rain began to fall, Sharon noticed the sky darkening. Soon, the rain turned to hail. Her daughter, Jessica, Lage's mother, called to warn her about the storm and urged her to get inside the store with the children to take shelter.

Inside the store, employees rushed the customers, including Rodney, to the employee training room near the rear of the store, where he and several others would take refuge under a table. Other customers stood around the perimeter of the training room.

Sharon, still in the parking lot, watched empty shopping carts roll north toward 20th Street. She went to push the door open so they could take shelter, but it wouldn't budge. It was almost like it was welded shut. She knew there was not enough time to do anything else and resolved that she could not change any possible outcome. Sharon placed the children on the floorboard behind the front seat of the pickup truck and laid across them with her back to the front window, holding them close. The children cried a little and they all began to pray to Jesus for safety. Mason felt pressure pushing down on her shoulders and opened her eyes to see a large person kneeling behind her in the pickup truck with his hands on her shoulders. She looked across to Lage and noticed another similarly dressed person, kneeling next to him, with his hands on Lage's shoulders as well. Mason noticed one of the two strangers had dark brown hair and the other had blond. She could see strapped sandals on their feet and wings folded behind them. She was not afraid. She knew both of the additional strangers in the pickup truck were angels and she had no doubt that they were going to survive the storm.

They felt the pickup truck hit the ground, not even realizing it had been lifted up. It crashed among broken shelves, mangled steel, and shattered concrete. The vehicle came to rest, facing north in the lawn and garden section, located in the front area of the store. The store's roof had collapsed onto the cab of the now nearly flattened pickup truck. Mason was impaled by a piece of angle iron from a steel girder that pierced through the roof and punctured her shoulder, exiting her back into the seat. Lage had serious head injuries. Sharon knew she was still in the vehicle, but the flattened roof and tremendous amount of debris kept her from seeing the back seat where Mason and Lage were seated just moments before. Mason and Sharon prayed, "God, please send somebody to come and help us quickly."

As soon as the storm was past, Rodney sought to get back to his wife and grandchildren in front of the store. Unable to get through the tangled debris inside the store, he climbed out over it, and through the back wall. He went around the collapsed building to reach the parking lot. At first, he could not find his pickup truck on the parking lot that was littered with wrecked cars. An employee suggested that maybe Sharon had seen the storm approaching and decided to drive to a safer place. It did not sound reasonable to Rodney, so he started looking through the debris. As he looked into the wreckage inside the front of the store, he caught a glimpse of a blue and white license plate that read "#1 Grandpa"—the license plate he proudly displayed on the back of his pickup truck was given to him by his grandchildren.

He worked his way around to the side of the mangled, flattened vehicle and found Lage on the ground beside the driver's door with massive head injuries. He stayed with Lage and comforted him until the emergency crews arrived. An ambulance attendant offered little hope in the prognosis for Lage due to the severity of his injuries. Because of the way Mason had been impaled by the roof beam, the steel girder had to be cut in front of and behind her to free her from the wreckage of the nearly-flattened pickup truck. She was transported to a hospital by ambulance in a sitting position with the beam left in place through her shoulder and back.

Both children went through extensive, complex surgeries at Freeman Hospital and were life-flighted to Children's Mercy Hospital in Kansas City, Missouri. Mason was released in early June and returned home. Lage's injuries were more severe. He spent 6 weeks in the hospital and required months of intense speech and physical therapy. Despite the trauma, both cousins are doing better than anyone had initially predicted.

◆ ◆ ◆

F red was at his home near the Wal-Mart store on 15th Street when the storm warning sirens sounded. He was always fascinated with storms and tornadoes. He had researched tornadoes and written papers on storms in college. Whenever he heard the storm warning sirens, he would usually drive over to the campus of Missouri Southern State University to watch the storms roll in. He particularly liked the view from the top of a hill on the visitor side of the football stadium. From there, he had a good view of the horizon over much of Joplin, Missouri. His wife, Linda, says it has been his routine for many years. If Fred would see a well-defined tornado, he often was inclined to follow it.

As the storm warning sirens sounded on that Sunday, Fred got into his car and headed for the football stadium. It seemed that there was nothing extraordinary about this storm. As he approached the first entrance to the stadium, he encountered a multitude of cars. He was not aware of the Joplin High School graduation ceremony being held on the campus that afternoon. The ceremony had just ended. There were cars everywhere and the lots were still full. Fred could not get to his preferred vantage point and so started home.

Fred was almost back to 7th Street on Duquesne Road when

he received a phone call from a friend in Branson, Missouri, telling him about the tornado warning sirens sounding in Joplin. Fred said that he was unable to get to his observation spot on the hill and was on his way home. When he walked through the front door of his house, he saw a KSNF weather report on the television in his living room. The tower camera was showing an image of the tornado on the ground. It was across town chewing up everything in its path. Fred watched as the storm on his television screen advanced through Joplin. He knew immediately that it was very serious. He walked into the bedroom where Linda was reading and told her to get up and change her shoes on immediately. She remembered one of the storm preparation tips from many years ago of putting on a heavy pair of shoes. She kicked off her sandals as Fred told her there was a huge tornado on the ground. Unsure of the precise location or direction, they would prepare for the worst.

Fred sent Linda to their son's bedroom to tell Tyler, and his friend who was visiting, to prepare for the storm. Linda, Tyler, and his friend gathered in the living room. Fred stepped out of the back door to see if there was any sign of the storm. He had no idea his house was in the direct line of the storm. When he looked west toward the back of Wal-Mart, he froze for a moment. The sky was as dark as night. He could see debris flying through the air just a couple blocks away, reminding him of a 3-D movie, with boards and other kinds of debris flying all around. Fred was concerned about the debris and was wondering exactly where the funnel cloud was. He figured the tornado must be somewhere south of his house. Except for all the airborne debris, he still did not think the tornado was really there. In actuality, it was only 2 blocks away. He went back into the house and told Linda, Tyler, and Tyler's friend that they needed to get into the narrow hallway located just off the living room in the center of the house.

As Linda and the boys were getting into the hallway, Fred

took one last look through a small window next to the front door. He could see shingles, wood, insulation, and other debris falling into the yard. Even then, Fred was unaware that the actual tornado was upon them. As they were standing in the hallway, Fred heard a "whoosh" as the whole house began to shake against a huge gust of wind. Linda could feel a rumbling and shaking coming from beneath the floor. They both realized this storm was different. They all knelt down on the floor in the hallway. The lights flickered a few seconds before the front wall of the storm slammed the house. Suddenly, the house seemed to literally explode around them. In an instant, they were all outside—except there was still the hallway floor underneath them. Tyler watched as a large section of the house spiraled upwards into the black sky. The house around them was gone, and they clung together in the elements, feeling the sting of heavy rain, cold hail, and assorted pieces of small debris. The pounding of debris was accompanied by a tremendous sound, similar to a jet engine taking off directly over their heads. The sound of twisting, bending, creaking metal, and the snapping and splintering of boards, the smashing and crashing glass, and loud explosions, was astounding. It surrounded them. Linda kept telling herself tornadoes are fast and furious and don't last long. However, on that day, the darkness and the incredibly loud noises felt endless.

Just before he got his head completely down for cover, Fred saw Linda's car that had been parked in the driveway land inside the footprint of the house about 7 feet from where they were all sitting with their arms and legs interlocked with each other for stability.

As they were sitting in the hallway, the pounding of the smaller debris was relentless. Fred knew that any single, large piece of debris could hit them at any time, and everything would be over. He was yelling to everyone over the loud noise of the wind and the debris to "hang on." As they were saying their goodbyes and going through all the associated emotions, Fred feared they would not make it through this storm alive. They were just trying to hang on however they could. The vacuum of the wind lifted them off the carpeted hallway floor. As Linda and Fred began to concede to what they believed to be their fate, their circumstances deteriorated. Tyler would later say that the more they resolved it was over, the farther they were all lifted off the floor. All of four them, intertwined together, were above the surface of the floor rotating slightly in place. Tyler's feet were up in the air, well above the level of the floor, and his father was doing his best to just hang onto him.

Tyler screamed out as loud as he could, "NO, GOD! PLEASE! It's not going to end this way. I have so much more to do with my life. I beg of You, and I beg for Your mercy. Whatever is Your will, but I don't want to go yet. I have so much more to do." Immediately, Tyler felt a force from behind him push them to the hallway floor.

After the winds of the storm had passed, Fred was able to stand to his feet and rejoice that they were all alive. Fred had Tyler and his friend take Linda to a neighbor's house a few doors north that was still standing to escape the hail and the lightning that followed the storm. As their house was located toward the northern wall of the storm, the initial winds from the southeast and east, took much of the debris from their house to the west and southwest. As Fred surveyed his surroundings from a field behind their property, he recognized nothing. His neighborhood was reduced to rubble.

When the storm had finally passed, only one room had any walls left standing and they were scarred by debris. Much of the contents and structure of the house were picked clean from the floor that remained. When they looked back at the spot in the hallway where they found refuge, they saw that only a small quantity of debris had been deposited there. That 5 by 7-foot area was nearly void of the debris that covered everything else, including the remaining master bathroom, despite how it had been lying in the open, unprotected from the wind for much of the time.

The living room couch was slammed and broken. Linda found steak knives from the wooden cutlery block on the kitchen counter, but many of the knives had been embedded in the back of the twisted couch.

Still, Linda was encouraged when she found the foot-long crucifix she had received when she was baptized many years prior. Their kitchen clock was pulled from the rubble with its hands at 5:46 p.m. Tyler found their basset hound wandering through the neighborhood about 30 minutes later; their two cats showed up 5 days later. Tyler's Social Security card was found in Diamond, Missouri several days after.

Fred and Linda were covered with massive bruises that seemed to worsen each day as more embedded debris would work themselves to the surface of the skin over the next few weeks. In light of the numerous airborne objects, including everything from 2x4s to cars, that narrowly missed them on the open floor of the hallway, both Linda and Fred considered themselves to be blessed with only minor injuries. It could very easily have been significantly worse, but for God's grace and protection. Fred tells of the many blessings he has noticed as a result of the storm. He has seen changes for the better in the lives of family and friends who have been confronted with the realities of this storm.

◆ ◆ ◆

R oger was standing on the east side of his home in Duquesne, Missouri on Sunday afternoon, discussing with his son, Trey, about where they should set up a basketball goal. They had not noticed any signs of ominous weather before that time, but they could only see the sky to the east of their home.

The woman who lived across the street from Roger yelled out to him that a tornado had destroyed St. John's Hospital and Joplin High School, and it was headed their way. With the sun still shining brightly at his home, Roger figured they were safe. After all, the hospital was 5 miles away and the high school was at least 3. Due to the distance, he was unconcerned. With his understanding of common storm tracks, he believed that he was too far east, too far south, and too far away. Surely, it would dissipate before it reached them.

Moments later, Roger realized he had underestimated the storm. He stuck his head out to look around the corner of his house to the west and saw a huge, dark cloud bearing down on their neighborhood. The color was somewhere between black, brown, and green, and it was devouring everything in sight. It was the biggest tornado he had ever seen. He figures the storm had already struck Academy Sports and Wal-Mart by the time he noticed it. He told Trey to go get the mattress from his bed and move into the middle bathroom. When Roger looked up at the huge cloud heading straight for them, he could see a section of chain link fence caught up in the wind about 100 feet in the air. He thought about getting under the house, but there was not enough time to make it there safely. As he was heading inside, Roger watched some of the shingles on a neighborhood home 2 blocks away start popping up in the air like popcorn. Seconds later, that house imploded and disappeared from sight.

Running through the living room into the safety of the bathroom, Roger passed a wall in the living room where a ceramic cross hung on a nail. The cross, for some reason, was always falling to the floor. If there was even the slightest commotion or bump in the room, Roger would have to pick the cross up off the floor and hang it back on the nail.

They were safely in the bathroom with just a few seconds to spare before the storm came blasting through the house.

The noises coming from the wind were tremendous. There were all kinds of debris smashing into everything around them. They could hear windows breaking and boards popping as they huddled together on the floor. It seemed like it went on for a long time, but it actually only lasted less than a minute before the calmness of the eye of the storm reached them. When the winds died down, Roger hugged his son and told him he loved him. They thought the storm had passed and the fury of the wind was over.

Roger opened the bathroom door and walked into the living room. He looked through the now glass-less frame of the living room window and snapped a picture of the front yard on his cell phone. After the front storm wall had passed, Roger saw his garage was still intact, as were most rooms of the house. The windows had all blown out. His double-glass patio doors had been carried into the living room. Like many people who experienced the eye of the storm, he too, thought the worst was over. He did not realize the most destructive winds were yet to come. Just after he snapped the picture on his phone, a blast of wind blew Roger back against an interior wall. He rushed back into the bathroom to the refuge of the mattress.

The house was thoroughly pounded by the back wall of the storm. The roof of the house, which survived the front half, peeled away. Roger could see the sky above him through the open ceiling in the bathroom. Chunks of debris swirled above their heads. He saw the undercarriage of a spinning vehicle as it was passing over them. The noise was incredibly loud. They could feel the battered walls of the house sway back and forth several times as if to purposefully break free of the foundation.

Roger was lying down on the floor underneath the mattress between the toilet and the bathtub, trying desperately to hang on. He jammed his feet against the bathroom door to keep it shut. Eventually, the sheer power of the wind pushed the door open, despite his efforts. What happened next was nothing short of miraculous and Roger believes it saved their lives. The wind created such force within the bathroom that it pulled the bottom drawer open on the bathroom vanity, a drawer that had been "stuck shut" for years—the family had given up on using the obstinate drawer. On that day, however, the wind forced the drawer open and held it at a fully extended position. The open drawer protruded from the face of the vanity and prohibited the bathroom door from opening more than a few inches. "It created a carburetor effect," Roger said. "Had that not happened, I think we both would have been pulled through the open ceiling by the vacuum in the storm."

Roger and Trey were praying to God and pleading for protection and deliverance from the terrorizing destructive winds. The noise was almost unbearable from the storm that was battering everything around them. The walls were shaking back and forth, being pummeled by the winds. Roger did not think the house could take much more pounding before it would suffer the same fate as the neighbor's house he saw a few minutes earlier.

Roger felt like the torment of the back half of the storm lasted several minutes, followed by several more minutes of pounding hail and pouring rain. When Roger was sure the storm had passed, he emerged from what was left of the bathroom to see the piles of rubble that, minutes earlier, were his home. There was not much left of Roger's house. The front half of the storm tore up some of the house. The back half of the storm pretty much finished the job. He and Trey had walked away unscathed with not even a scratch between them and were thankful they had been brought through the seemingly endless fury of the storm.

By the time the storm had finished ravaging the neighborhood, it had left behind enormous piles of debris. Roger's shattered house was absent the garage, his bedroom, the spare bedroom, the den, half the kitchen, his daughter's bedroom, and the second bathroom. About two-thirds of the house was just gone, most of the remaining rooms were missing large sections of either internal and/or exterior walls, and what was left had no roof. Some ceiling joists remained. The winds coming mainly out of the west had pushed Roger's car about 30 feet, into where the garage had been standing before the storm.

The ceramic cross that was always falling to the floor was still hanging on the nail, unfazed by the storm. The wall on which it hung was now freestanding and riddled with scars from flying debris. The cross had fallen from the wall so many times in the past after even the slightest movement in the room. Yet, somehow it managed to stay on its nail as most of the wall around it was ripped from the floor and ceiling. Seeing it there brought a sense of peace to them both.

"God decided to leave that cross there on that wall as a reminder," Roger said. "It would be difficult for somebody to look closely at everything that went on that day and still believe there is no God."

Roger and Trey grabbed their first aid kit, and with the help of several of their neighbors, assisted in pulling 11 people safely from the wreckage of their homes in the neighborhood.

CHAPTER 15
GUIDANCE AND DIRECTION

"Now an angel of the Lord said to Philip, 'Go south to the road—the desert road—that goes down from Jerusalem to Gaza.'"—**Acts 8:26 (NIV)**

"The chief priest and the whole party of the Sadducees who were with him were extremely jealous. So they took action by arresting the apostles and putting them in the city jail. But at night an angel from the Lord opened the doors to their cell and led them out of the prison."—**Acts 5:17-19 (GW)**

P atty was driving south on Maiden Lane to St. John's Hospital to take her friend, Anthony, in for his breathing treatments. The torrential rain brought the visibility down to about a block as they approached the hospital. By the time they reached 23rd Street, the strong winds were beginning to seriously blow the car around. They watched as the sky quickly turned darker.

They knew the worsening conditions were a strong indication that something bad could happen, but they had no idea the front wall of the tornado was closing in on them fast. Patty began to speed up to get to the safety of the hospital, only a couple blocks away. By the time they reached the entrance to the hospital emergency room, the wind-driven rain had brought visibility to nearly nothing. Over the resonances of pounding wind, hail, and torrential rain, neither heard the warning sound of storm sirens.

Patty could not find an open parking place between the helicopter landing pad and the front doors of the emergency room. Pulling her small, Ford Focus into the circle drive in front of the emergency room entrance, she hoped to let Anthony out as near to the building as possible. There was a dark SUV parked just in front the emergency room doors, facing east. Noticing it would be difficult to drive around it, she was trying to decide what to do when her car was hit with the first huge blast of wind coming out of the south. She decided to pull up behind the SUV and parked her car facing the oncology department, immediately south of the circle drive about 50 feet from the front door of the emergency room. The wind and the rain momentarily eased up.

Patty and Anthony decided to get out of the car during the brief break in the wind and rain. Patty sensed in her spirit that something was not right. A clear and concise inner voice was telling her to "get in the car and stay in the car, and you will be safe."

"Get back into the car," she heard again.

They quickly got back into the car and closed the doors as the winds started picking back up. The wind, blowing directly from the south, immediately strengthened. They had no time to notice that a large tornado was devouring the office buildings across the street. The rain and the hail began falling nearly horizontal, parallel to the ground. The visibility was reduced to almost nothing. Anthony pressed Patty down under the dash as far as she was able to go. The windows on the car immediately blew out, either from the pounding hail or the wind-driven debris. Anthony lay over the top of Patty to cover her as the small car started rocking violently back and forth. Patty thought the wind was going to last forever.

The wind direction shifted quickly as the storm encountered the sturdy outside structure of the hospital. The heaviest wind was pounding the car from the southeast on Patty's side. There was no break or letting up of the incredible force of the wind. They both began to wonder how long it would be before the small car would be propelled by the wind. As the car was rocking back and forth, they could not understand how it could possibly stay on the ground. Through the wind and the noise, scared as they both were, there was a sense of peace that came over them. They understood that it could only be the "Hand of God" that held them there.

The intense winds had picked up a tremendous volume of debris by the time it reached St. John's Hospital. The air was filled with broken glass, splintered wood, gravel, insulation, dirt, and other debris. The unimaginable force of the 200 mile per hour winds was sandblasting everything its path. As Patty and Anthony sat cowering for protection from the storm, all they could do was pray. "We prayed to God for forgiveness of what we were and how we were," Anthony said. Patty was yelling, "Jesus, Jesus," over the roar of the storm. As instantly as the violent storm winds started, they stopped, at least for a moment or so as the central eye of the massive storm passed directly overhead.

Anthony could see up into the eye of the storm as it passed over them. He noted that the sky above the inside of the funnel was crystal clear blue; free of the black debris that had been carried in the face of the storm wall that had just passed. He watched many small, shiny white things floating calmly around inside of the eye of the tornado. "They looked like people clothed in white coats or white robes just floating around," Anthony said.

As quickly as the front face of the storm left, the back wall came roaring in. The chaos from the wind and the debris seemed endless. They were pounded ruthlessly by hail and debris as they hunkered down inside what was left of the battered car. Finally, the wind died down, the hail got smaller, then stopped, and the rain decreased considerably. By the grace of God, they had made it through.

Patty and Anthony sat in the beaten, windowless Ford Focus. The car had acted like a funnel and was filled with glass, gravel, sticks, branches, shredded fragments of asphalt shingles, and pieces of splintered wood. Patty's closed purse was filled with debris, as was her laptop computer that sat on the back seat. There was so much force to the debris inside the car that the gearshift knob was twisted on itself. The outside of the car had taken a terrible beating, but was intact. The car looked as if it had been sandblasted from top to bottom. A large piece of steel that they believed was part of the building's roof had been hurled by the wind through the front windshield. It miraculously came to a complete stop a foot and a half short of hitting Anthony directly in the head.

Anthony had some minor scratches on his arm and behind his ear. He exited the car with no trouble. Patty was unable to get her driver's door open, so she climbed across to get out through the open passenger's door. She walked away without a scratch. As they climbed out of the wrecked remains of the car, they saw that the parking lot had been emptied; no vehicles remained around them. All the cars had been picked up by the tremendous winds, tossed, smashed, and stacked into large piles beyond the wrecked shell of a St. John's Hospital helicopter that lay on its side about 40 yards behind them.

Neither Patty nor Anthony realized they had actually gone through a tornado. They both thought it was a big windstorm that drove the debris and the heavy rains. The realization that it was indeed a massive tornado did not begin to sink in until they took a good look at what was left around them. They saw all the trees at Cunningham Park, across 26th Street to the north, were gone. The local Pronto store at the corner of 26th Street and Maiden Lane looked like nothing more than a pile of bricks. The doctors' buildings to the west of the hospital looked like they had been leveled by a bomb. Other than the window-less hospital beside them, there was nothing left standing. Finally, recognizing the awesome power of the storm, they felt a sense of awe that they were alive. There was a sense of peace because they were spared. They were not traumatized or terribly shaken.

They walked towards the window-less frames of the emergency room door. The SUV that had been parked in front of them was blown into the lobby of the emergency room. All the furniture and the reception desk area had been pushed further into the building. There were large piles of debris around and inside the entrance. There was the strong smell of natural gas. Water was pouring from the ceiling onto floors that were covered with debris and shattered glass. There were people asking for help to get freed from the debris that blew down through the emergency room halls. After Patty and Anthony left the hospital, about 20 minutes after the storm, they walked over to the Ozark Center, New Directions office, east of the hospital to see if they could assist some of the people who might need help there.

Looking back, Patty and Anthony are amazed there were not more injuries and casualties. They attributed it to God and the many people who prayed for His protection.

"We should not have made it through that evening," Patty said. "It had to be the protective Hand of God that surrounded us."

Had there been one open parking place, they may have ended up parking away from the shelter the building provided. Had they not heeded the inner voice to get back into the car, things may not have gone well for them. They realize that being in a very small car in the path of such a powerful storm was probably one of the worst places to look for shelter. But, as it turned out, it was likely better than anywhere else they would have found on their own. The lightweight car should have, at the very least, been pushed all over the parking lot. The SUV that was parked in front of the door kept them from pulling closer to the building. They both feel that there must be a larger plan for them. Both have a renewed outlook and afterward went on to work with other people to help them cope with the realities of the May 22 storm.

◆ ◆ ◆

J errad had just finished picking up a few things at the 15th Street Wal-Mart and decided it was time to head for home; it was about 5 p.m. when he got into his pickup truck to begin the drive across town to his grandparent's home. He noticed the sky was getting very dark to the southwest but did not give it too much thought. Even the dark clouds looming ahead of him as he drove home did not cause much concern. It seemed no different than the dozens of thunderstorms that he could remember. His trip across town was uneventful. As he pulled his pickup truck into the garage, a few blocks east of St. John's Hospital, storm warning sirens began to sound.

Jerrad went upstairs in the 100-year-old house and was thinking about playing a video game as he might do on any other Sunday afternoon. With the storm warning siren still sounding in the background, Jerrad turned on the television and heard a weather bulletin announcing a tornado on the ground. He did not catch where the announcer said the tornado was or where it was headed, but it still did not seem to be urgent at the time. It was probably somewhere else anyway.

Jerrad walked downstairs without any urgency. Just after he reached the ground floor, the lights flickered off and on a couple of times before going completely dark. As he made his way to the basement stairway, he began to hear a dull roar outside the house. He did not associate the sound with the tell-tale "freight train" noise of a tornado, but rather a low, constant roll of thunder. When he had reached the bottom of the basement stairs, he heard a window break on one of the floors above him. He could tell from the muted light coming through the basement window that it had gotten much darker outside. Jerrad realized that it was truly a tornado, and it was right on top of him. The noise was growing considerably louder but was not deafening.

The older home was built on a hillside that sloped down to the east. The basement design was somewhere between a full underground structure and a walkout design. The slope of the hill was not steep enough for the walls to allow a walk-out entrance, but the slope was steep enough that the exterior walls on the low side of the hill exposed the top two-thirds of the basement wall. What resulted was a basement wall that was concrete up to 2 feet above the floor. The top 6 feet of the exterior downhill wall was constructed as a normal, exterior, wooden frame wall. The western wall of the house, on the uphill side of the house was more like a full in-ground concrete basement. The wall on that side of the basement was solid concrete from the basement floor all the way to the floor joists above. The north and south walls were partially concrete and wood frame exterior construction. The concrete in those two walls reached higher than the 2-foot-high knee-wall level in the east wall, but not as high as the 8-foot level in the west wall.

With the power out, the house was very dark in the basement; little light was filtering through the windows with the monstrous storm cloud bearing down on the house. Jerrad felt he was somehow being directed to go to a specific spot, about 20 feet from the steps in the southwest corner near the exterior wall. Of all the basement walls to choose, this one had the lowest height of concrete structure. Jerrad did not see a physical arrow directing him to go to the spot and stand, but later said, "There might as well have been one." There was a strong sense that he needed to get to that precise, particular spot and no other place, and stand next to that wall. "I just knew that I needed to go there," Jerrad said, indicating that the commanding voice in his head demanded that he, "Get over there and stand there and nowhere else, now!"

There was nothing particularly different about that location in the basement from any other place in the room. Jerrad hurried toward the wall as he heard a large crash, as if one of the walls upstairs had fallen in. He was able to get to the particular spot next to the short concrete wall and he stood up straight, a few feet away from the wall. He did not bend over, or crouch down, or even cover his head.

Only 5 seconds had elapsed since Jerrad first heard the upstairs window break before the first burst of the storm pounded the house. As soon as Jerrad reached the "safe spot" the entire house above him imploded; the tornado destroying everything that had been overhead. He was not aware of any excessive noise or even a crash. It seemed like he blinked, and it was unceremoniously gone.

The house was located near the southern edge of the storm wall. The initial winds struck the house from the southwest side, the same corner of the basement where Jerrad was standing. The debris from the two-story house were blown east and north from the foundation. The roof and the top floor of the house landed in the yard just a short distance away, northeast of the now exposed basement. The first-floor structure collapsed and ended up in the basement, filling most of the space with debris.

When Jerrad looked at the wall behind him, the wooden portion of the exterior wall was also gone. All that remained was the 2-foot-tall, concrete knee-wall a few feet behind him. It had all been cleanly removed from the concrete base. There was not even a small piece of debris that had fallen within 10 feet of where he stood. It all ended up farther away. Even the wood frame wall that had been within arm's reach behind him had been picked up and moved away, without any consequence to

Jerrad. The debris was everywhere around him. The area where he was standing was clear. He received no injuries from the debris, not even a minor scratch or a bruise. The stairway to the upstairs ground floor was ripped out of the basement. The debris in the basement seemed to have an extraordinary number of electrical lines and wires that crisscrossed everywhere.

The wind speed had died down tremendously, allowing him to concentrate on his next plan of action. The rain poured down on Jerrad as he stood there, barefoot, in the basement. The wall did nothing to protect him from the wind and rain. With nothing but a knee-high barrier behind him, he just stepped out over the short wall and ran barefoot across the street, navigating large amounts of debris and downed power lines, to a brick structure that was still standing and seemed relatively intact. All the other houses in the neighborhood were either severely damaged or gone.

Jerrad believes that, if he had stayed upstairs, he probably would not have heard anything over the sound of the air conditioner. There were only a few moments of time after hearing the storm warning on the television before the power went out. Looking back, Jerrad felt like an unseen force guided him to the safety near the inconspicuous 2-foot-tall concrete knee-wall. He knows that there is a reason that things happened as they did. There are too many things that could have gone terribly wrong for him. There was no extra time to spare with the same results. Any minor delay or indecision would have likely ended with much more somber consequences. Jerrad admits that, even though he was scared, he felt as if he was in a protective bubble.

◆ ◆ ◆

May 22 started like any other Sunday for Karen, and her husband, Chris. They attended morning services at

Harvest Time Assembly of God church south of Carthage, Missouri. That morning, when the pastor asked if anyone had a testimony, Karen stood up and said, "As for me and my house, we will stand up and serve the Lord, no matter what." Little did she know that would be tested in only a few hours.

It was a warm day, predicted to reach the 90s that afternoon. Karen and Chris had their house, located east of Joplin High School, closed with the air conditioning on. They heard the storm warnings on the television like so many other people that day. Chris was in their front yard when the second warning siren sounded. He could see the greenish gray wall approaching from the southwest and knew that meant hail was on the way. There was not any rain there at that time. He did not notice a funnel or debris visible in the storm. Karen yelled to him to get out of the weather and he turned to do so; believing that it would be nothing more than a strong hailstorm. Wind increasing, the couple struggled with the front door, working to close it before Karen locked it.

The wind started whistling through the house. Standing in the middle of their south-facing living room, they could hear debris hitting the outside walls of their home as some of their windows began breaking. The rain, falling nearly horizontally, poured in through the broken windows. The room immediately became dark, and the noise intensified as Karen followed Chris toward the bathroom.

Karen looked back long enough to see holes opening in the walls as debris punched through not only the outside walls, but ripped through the interior walls as well. There would be many large holes punched into and out of the living room walls before Karen was able to get out of the living room into the hallway. "It was like Pop... Pop, Pop... Pop. Pop... Pop," Karen said. The debris moved so fast through the room that Karen could not see what it was. She said, "It was like a science fiction movie or a horror movie; very surreal. The holes were just showing up. The curtain blowing in the wind from the broken window would stand out as it would get hit by debris, followed instantly by another hole across the room."

Chris estimated that only about 30 seconds had elapsed since he first saw the green cloud from his front yard. It was very close. As he passed his bedroom door, he recalled hearing the window break and thought his bed was going to get wet. He still thought that this was just a hailstorm with some wind. There was no reality of a funnel in his mind yet.

By the time they got to the bathroom door the noise became overwhelming. "It was similar to what you would experience if you were being shelled in wartime," Chris said. Karen had been around several tornadoes before and described the noise as, "A spooky, grounding, growl." The growl was so loud they could not tell what was going on. The strongest wind had not even reached the front of the house yet. It was still a few seconds away.

As they reached the bathroom door, Karen felt God speak to her spirit telling her, "No! Not here! Go there!" She looked ahead and could see a forearm and hand pointing toward the closet in a middle bedroom. She describes the sense as, "Go here! Don't go to any of those others! Here! Go here!" Karen told Chris not to stop in the bathroom but go to that closet instead. When Chris asked why, Karen told him that she saw an arm pointing toward the closet. Chris said that answer was good enough for him. He agreed that, wherever they were going, they were going together, "Like two peas in a pod." They reached the closet that had no doors on it. It was small, only about 2 by 5-foot and was packed with off-season clothes. There was a window in the bedroom facing the north, away from the wind. They squeezed together and backed into the closet.

Chris and Karen had started praying and praising God as they passed the bathroom door. Karen said she didn't feel anxious, nor was she scared. They didn't feel anything. Karen's claustrophobia would have kept her from the closet on any other given day, but it was not an issue during the storm. She did not remember anything but praying and praising. She doesn't remember hearing anything different after she reached the closet as compared to when the storm first started.

They were standing together, backed into the closet one moment, and then they were laying down the next moment. Chris believes that when the roof peeled away, the closet tilted, and they slid down. As the unsupported structure of the closet started to fall slowly toward the floor, a cushion shot from the couch across the room and landed underneath them, cushioning their fall. An afghan from the couch also blew across the room and covered their heads, protecting their faces. There was a lot of debris flying around them, leaving a pile just outside the closet entrance. Other than being covered in mud and a fiberglass-insulation mix, they were spared any injuries other than a couple of bruises. The closet was the only place that offered solid protection.

Because their home was out of the eye of the tornado which passed by about 2 blocks to the north, there was no break in the action for them. The wind that initially reached them came out of the south to southwest. The leading edge of the front shifted around to come out of the north to northwest by the time it was finished.

When the wind stopped, there was a dense, dark, blackness that was quickly followed by frigid rain and hail. The temperature dropped from nearly 90 degrees before the storm to what felt like 45 to 50 degrees. Chris lifted Karen out of the small area and helped her down off what was left of the house. The bathroom that they had initially stepped toward for shelter was gone. There were even places where the subfloor in the bathroom was peeled up and Chris could see the ground below the floor where the tub had set not more than 5 minutes before.

There is no doubt of what their fate would have been had they chosen not to follow the hand that guided them.

They could see fire at Franklin Technology Center, just a few blocks due west from them. To get out of the cold rain and pounding hail, they headed for their car. Before the storm, the car was parked in the driveway facing north, but was now up against the front porch facing 180 degrees away, toward the south. Its rear axle broke when the car was thrown backwards into the concrete porch. All the windows were out. Chris's truck, used for his surveying business, was moved about 50 to 60 feet. They waited out the hailstorm inside the shell of the car.

When the hailstorm was over, Karen and Chris got out of the car. Within minutes, many people were walking aimlessly, as if in a stupor, asking where they were or how to get to some place. Karen saw packs of animals—cats and dogs running together—first up the street, then down the street, back and forth several times. Then she never saw them again. First responders showed up within minutes of the storm.

Karen and Chris lost almost everything in their home. Items not taken in the wind, or ruined in the rain or debris, were rendered unusable by mold, with one major exception. Chris operated his business out of his home, but his records and computer in the garage were protected when the outside wall of the garage fell over his file cabinets, holding them down and keeping the rain out.

Even with the needed decompression and occasional emotional moment, they maintain that they have been blessed immensely since the storm. Karen frequently tells people she comes into contact with that she is, "Alive because God."

"The blessings didn't stop when God saved us," Chris said.

Blessings continued when Jeff, the couple's insurance agent, arrived a few days after the storm. He offered them so much more comfort and support than they anticipated. Jeff asked how they were doing. Chris said, "We are great. Praise the Lord." Jeff asked if they were Christians and if he could pray with them. "It is not our normal policy," Jeff continued, "but we are out in the street and I can do it."

Chris' son called him a few days later to set up a meeting with several men from Kenneth Copeland Ministries. They came by to pray with Chris and Karen, listen to their testimony, and offer further assistance. A few weeks later, the ministry sent a package including a leather bound, "Spirit Filled Bible" to replace the one Chris lost. Later, a survey company from Virginia called Chris to donate two truckloads of survey equipment, supplies, computers, and software from the downsizing of their business. They also gave him a truck. Chris and Karen said God used many people to replace everything lost with something better. Chris was able to pay his blessings forward and donated his old truck to one of his competitors, another surveyor, in town. We found out later that the competitor would go on to donate his old truck to another company as well, continuing to spread the blessings.

◆ ◆ ◆

When the storm sirens sounded, Tina was taking her time mowing her back yard while her husband, Mark, trimmed and edged the front lawn of their home near 22nd Street and Connecticut Avenue. They did not notice anything unusual in the sky. There were some storm clouds building off to the west, but nothing seemed unusual. They felt no sense of urgency or impending danger. Tina finished the mowing before the couple went into the house and cleaned up.

The second siren caught their attention. Tina rounded up her three children—Alicia, 15, Jacob, 11, and Hannah, 10—and they sat on the floor in the hallway, with the family dog. Mark was not concerned and did not join them immediately. He, like many, had grown accustomed to hearing sirens that preceded non-weather events.

The rain began to pick up a little, but still nothing seemed unusual. Wind coming out of the southwest prompted Mark to walk to the front door to see if there was anything different going on outside. He opened the glass security door a little so he could get a better view of the worsening weather. The second warning siren had stopped about a minute earlier. It never crossed his mind that the storm siren stopped because the approaching storm destroyed the system. For all he knew, the warning had expired, and they would only have to wait out the heavy rain. The sky grew dark, and the wind picked up dramatically. The rain began to blow horizontally toward the north.

Mark watched as several of the neighbor's trees began to topple. In just an instant, the front glass security door was ripped from his grip, torn from its hinges, and thrown into the front yard. Tina ran from the hallway to help, combining their efforts to get the main door closed and secured. They ran into the hallway and huddled with their children. The tornado was about a block away. Within seconds, the full force of the destructive winds was upon them. All of them were on the floor sandwiched together. Tina could hear each member of her family praying. The prayers sounded like a constant chatter that would continue until the storm passed and the wind and rain stopped. Mark laid over Tina and their children to protect them as best he could.

As the force of the high winds smashed into the house, large parts of the roof and ceiling were torn off. Broken glass had all blown into the rooms and hallway where the family huddled together. Pictures that had lined the hallway walls began to fall on top of them as the house shook violently. The sound of the wind outside was almost a deafening roar. It did not stop or subside until the storm had completely passed. Even though it was no longer than a few minutes from beginning to end, Tina said it felt like the storm's roar went on for half an hour. Mark was trying to hold the bedroom doors and the bathroom door shut to protect them from the flying shards of glass and debris. The louvers on the attic fan above them rattled loudly as the wind screamed through what was left of the attic. With sections of the roof missing, and the winds blowing through the broken windows, the pressure inside the house seemed to be lessened. They did not feel like they were in danger of being lifted from the floor by the low pressure of the storm—gusts of wind were pulling at them and over them, but not from underneath. The floor seemed secure. Despite the chaos, Tina felt a certain peace that her family would make it through the storm safely.

In the midst of the storm, Hannah got up from the family huddle and headed toward the bathroom door, just behind them. She wanted to get into the bathtub because she believed it was the safest place to be in a tornado. An audible voice told Tina not to go into that bathroom and to keep the family together in the hallway, so she stopped Hannah. "It felt as if God had His Hand over us in the hallway and we should stay put exactly where we were." They would be safer where they were. There was no doubt in Tina's mind that the floor in the hallway was the exact place that she, Mark, and their children were supposed to be. The family rode out the rest of the storm on the floor in the hallway. When the wind, rain, and hail had stopped, they opened the bathroom door to see that a very large tree limb had crashed through the outside wall of the bathroom and pierced the bathtub. Had any of them sought protection in the tub, the results would most likely have been tragically different.

When they emerged from the battered home, Tina said the sense of peace was still present, even as they saw the tremendous amount of damage in the neighborhood.

A few days later, after the rains had stopped, they received assistance from a group of volunteers affiliated with Samaritan's

Purse. The group came to the neighborhood to assist families in cleanup and recovery of their belongings. The volunteers were just like numerous other groups, helpings families in neighborhoods across the city. Within 3 hours, the men had the debris hauled to the street and a tarp covering what remained of the roof. Ladies from the group were cleaning the broken glass near the front door.

As the women worked around the front porch, they found a torn piece of the front cover of a leather-bound Holy Bible that had become plastered to the wall adjacent to the front door of the home. Shortly later, they also found a photograph of a church sanctuary that had come to rest in the corner of the deck on the back of the house. They found no other pictures or similar pieces in any other debris and neither Mark nor Tina recognized the items. Tina felt encouragement, comfort, peace, and calm with these items, that serve as reminders of the family's deliverance through the tremendous storm.

Before they would go to the next house, the volunteer group left Mark and Tina with a bucket of supplies and personal items that would be of great value in the coming days. Tina and Mark felt encouraged as the group of total strangers came into their lives, helped them pick up the broken pieces, and then sat down in a circle on their front yard to pray for and with Mark, Tina, and their children. They blessed the house, the family, and then blessed and presented a Bible to Mark and Tina, filled with signed, personal notes from the volunteers.

The family lost a lot of material things, but came back stronger morally and spiritually.

CHAPTER 16
COMFORT

"'How can I talk to you, sir? I have no strength left, and the wind has been knocked out of me.'

"Again, the person who looked like a human touched me, and I became stronger. He said, 'Don't be afraid. You are highly respected. Everything is alright! Be strong! Be strong!'

"As he talked to me, I became stronger. I said, 'Sir, tell me what you came to say. You have strengthened me.'"—**Daniel 10:17-19 (GW)**

"Then an angel appeared to Him from heaven, strengthening Him."—**Luke 22:43 (NKJV)**

E mily, 12, gathered with her family on May 22, 2011, to see her brother, Joe, graduate from high school. The ceremony for the Joplin High School was held at the Leggett and Platt Athletic Center on the campus of Missouri Southern State University that Sunday afternoon. Her parents, Kenny and Diane, and her 8-year-old brother and sister, twins Michael and Maggie, also traveled across town to see Joe graduate. Emily's older brother, Taylor, his wife, Andrea, and their 2-year-old daughter, Ella, were there too.

About halfway through the ceremony, after Joe had walked across the stage to receive his diploma, Taylor and Andrea decided to go ahead and leave—Ella was getting restless, so they offered to take her back to Kenny and Diane's home, located near St. Mary's Catholic Church, across town. The rest of the family would meet them when the ceremony was over. Emily got up as if she was going to leave with Taylor and his family, but then hesitated. For some reason, she went back and sat down with her parents. None of them were aware of any storm warnings.

After the ceremony was over, Emily and her family spent some time taking pictures of Joe and his friends. When they finished, Emily climbed into the family Suburban for the ride home. She sat in the bucket seat directly behind her father. Michael sat in the bucket seat next to Emily, behind his mother. Maggie sat in the third-row bench seat by herself. Neither Michael nor Maggie were using car seats. As they were preparing to leave the university, the first storm warning siren sounded. They all looked around at the sky and saw nothing unusual. There were some darker clouds off in the distance to the southwest, but nothing seemed out of the ordinary. The sky looked just like it did before any other storm. As the sirens continued to scream, they quickened their pace.

The weather report on the car radio told of severe weather approaching. On the way home, Kenny decided to stop and purchase gas. He pulled into the Kum and Go at the corner of 7th Street and Duquesne Road. Diane suggested that he only put 5 dollars worth of gas in the tank, so they would not waste any time getting home.

The sky was growing considerably darker. For some reason, Kenny put 20 dollars worth of gas into the tank. It delayed their departure by a few extra minutes. Weather bulletins were suggesting the storm would go north of Joplin. The announcer mentioned Riverton, Kansas, Asbury, Missouri, and Carl Junction, Missouri as being in the path of the storm. Nobody knew there were two tandem storms that would merge together just west of Joplin and cut a path right through the middle of town. Kenny and Diane still believed the storm would bypass them. As they were sitting at the gas station, Emily rolled down her window, resting her arm on the frame, she felt several very large raindrops hit her. "Mom told me once, that big raindrops sometimes come with tornadoes," Emily thought to herself. She shook the thought from her mind.

They headed west on 7th Street toward Range Line Road. The dark clouds that were building to the south and west were now clearly visible. Diane hesitated, then asked Kenny to get off 7th Street, remembering the tornado that had gone through Joplin in the early 1970s. Even though that tornado had first touched down near 26th Street on Schifferdecker Avenue and cut a path past Missouri Southern, much of the visible damage was on East 7th Street. Kenny turned south on Illinois Avenue and ended up on Indiana Avenue, going past Joplin High School. By the time they turned west on 26th Street, the sky was almost black. Emily told her mother she was scared—Diane agreed. The weather conditions worsened. They were unable to distinguish any cloud rotation or debris through the rain and had no idea they were headed directly into the storm. The storm was about to ravage St. John's Hospital, 2 miles to the west, and would reach them in no time.

When they came to the intersection at the corner of 26th and Main Streets, the conditions had improved slightly. The sky was still black, but the driving rain had stopped. They had to wait behind a truck stopped for a red light. It seemed like it took forever for the light to change to green. In those few moments, Diane noticed a large white decal on the back glass of the truck. The picture was a silhouette depicting a bowed head with a crown of thorns—the face of Jesus. The image stuck in Diane's mind.

The rain began to fall again. It was much worse than before. Kenny was impatiently asking aloud why the man would not just go ahead and drive through the red light. While they sat there waiting for the light to change, Emily decided to unbuckle her seatbelt. She knew she would not have much time to get out of the car and into the house. The 1 or 2 seconds she saved now could give her a little bit more time at home. When they looked back on the events, the time saved would make no difference, but the released seatbelt may have changed the ultimate outcome for Emily. Finally, the light turned green. Kenny sped around the truck, determined to get his family to safety. They would be home in less than a minute.

By the time Kenny passed Wall Avenue, near Irving Elementary School, the wind picked up dramatically. As he looked ahead in the direction of St. John's Hospital, he could see the bright blue flashes of exploding transformers. Diane had turned to comfort Emily, Michael, and Maggie, when a large piece of hail or debris struck and shattered the side window next to Maggie. Diane screamed for the children to get down. In that moment of screaming out to the children, Diane glanced out the passenger's side window to see The GreenBriar elderly care facility. The Suburban had become airborne. In the next instant, all the windows shattered. Emily reached back to grab Maggie's hand as she lay down in the seat behind her. Emily tried to cover her own head to shield it from the debris flying through the Suburban by holding Joe's diploma next to her face. They crashed to a stop, only a block away from their home.

Diane doesn't know when the Suburban became airborne, or how high it went, but it crashed down and came to rest on its wheels against the two steel posts supporting the sign for Dr. Pat Thompson's dental practice, west of The GreenBriar elderly care facility. The force of the crash and the winds buckled the steel beams and doubled the sign over onto the top of the wrecked Suburban. Debris was still pummeling them from all directions. Emily later said the process reminded her of a bad roller coaster ride she thought would never end.

Emily felt a tremendous crash as a very large piece of debris slammed against the driver's side of the car. The impact was so great that the diploma she had used to shield her face and head was knocked out of her hands and blown away. Emily compares the intense noise to the sound of driving down the interstate at 70 miles per hour with the windows open, but louder—much,

much louder.

A large piece of sheet metal ended up covering Maggie as she lay down in the back seat. She, like everyone else, was covered with shards of wood, shingles, and other debris. Kenny had a large gash on his side and his back. Everybody in the car was covered with cuts. Maggie needed stitches on her back. Emily had a large 9-inch-long gash on her left thigh. A large chunk of flesh had been carved from her leg, leaving her femur bone exposed.

After the winds stopped, Kenny and Diane began to climb out of the crumpled Suburban. They were forced to get back inside the vehicle as hail began to fall. When they finally got out of the vehicle, they saw Dr. Thompson's office, about 30 yards to the north, with the garage doors on the lower level ripped from their frames. They thought there might be enough room inside to allow for shelter. They could not see anything else around them still standing. The GreenBriar facility, about 20 yards away, was nearly flat. There were massive piles of debris as far as they could see. Diane grabbed the twins, and Kenny reached through the open window to lift Emily and carry her to shelter.

The first thing Emily saw as she was lifted out through the window was the large cross standing in front of St. Mary's Church a block away. Diane described it as just staring down on top of them and recalls that signs from God were all around them. It brought comfort even in the midst of the turmoil. "The doors of Heaven were opened to allow the angels to come through," Diane said, "and the angels came, and they came, and they came. They came in spirit form, and they came in human form... they were all around us that night."

When they reached Dr. Thompson's office, there was so much debris blocking their way they had a hard time getting inside, but Kenny was able to move some of the larger pieces. They would eventually move into an adjacent room where there would be more room for Emily to lay down while Kenny went for help. Diane and the twins stayed by Emily's side. When Emily closed her eyes, she felt a calmness. When she opened her eyes, she became acutely aware of the screams, the sirens, the smoky smell, and the pain. When she closed her eyes, those senses would be again replaced by calm and peace. She was on the floor inside the office for about an hour or so.

Emily felt a calming hand rest on her left shoulder. It was accompanied by a voice saying to her, "Everything is going to be alright." Emily would later describe the hand as being present for just awhile. However, she would describe the voice as being, "Equivalent to a whole conversation, lasting much longer than just one sentence." Earlier, as she lay there with her eyes closed, she was aware of the darkness of her closed eyelids. When she felt the presence of the hand on her shoulder, she could see a brightness piecing the darkness through her closed eyelids. From that point forward, for the rest of the night, Emily felt as if she were wrapped in a blanket of peace. She knew that she was going to be alright. Even as everything around Emily was chaotic, a sense of peace stayed with her. She does not have the words to describe how calming and peaceful it felt. She believes that normally, under these circumstances, she would be crying, screaming, or freaking out, but things were different, 180 degrees different. There was no drama for Emily that day. There were no bruises or marks on her shoulder where the hand was felt.

Though Emily had not seen the wound on her leg, she was aware of the puddle of blood beneath her. Kenny left to go see if he could find a car to get Emily to a hospital. He ran to his house to see if he could get the other family car out of the garage, only to discover that the house had been severely damaged, and their car was nowhere to be found. While Diane and Emily sat on the floor inside the office, a woman they believed to be a nurse on her way to work happened by. She helped them put a tourniquet on Emily's leg to stop the bleeding. Diane had no idea how the woman was able to find them. They were inside a destroyed building, in a walkout basement room, amid destruction as far as a person could see in any direction, in the middle of what resembled a war zone. How did the woman end up with them? How could she have even found them? The woman looked Diane straight in the face and told her to stay with Emily. Neither Diane nor Emily recalled seeing the woman leave. She was just gone. As she stayed with Emily, Maggie took Emily by the hand and sang *"Twinkle, Twinkle, Little Star."* It was so uplifting to Emily and she had no doubt that she was going to be alright.

Kenny had been unable to find a car to get Emily to a hospital but brought some blankets from the house to keep her warm, then went in search of a car again. He met up with a neighbor who had been with them at the graduation ceremony earlier that day. They gave him the keys to their car. Kenny drove toward Emily; though she was only a few blocks away, he was unable to get through the debris field blocking the streets.

While at his house earlier, Kenny had talked to his neighbor, Matthew, who said he had a medical supply bag and might be able to help Emily. When Matthew arrived at the office, he opened the bag to find that he had grabbed the wrong bag. It was full of baseball and sports equipment instead. They realized that, because of the scope of the damage in the area, they would probably be there awhile before anybody would come to their assistance. There were plenty of things in the area to keep the paramedics, firefighters, and police occupied with the flattened, elderly care facility on the next block. They decided to move Emily themselves. Matthew picked up Emily to carry her out of the wrecked office and do what he could to get her to a hospital. As he picked her up, Emily recalled the nice smell of his cologne. It was a welcome break from the combination of the acrid smell of smoke from burning wreckage, the heavy blanket of natural gas fumes, and the musty smell of the debris. She had pieces of asphalt shingles, insulation, and other debris in her hair, nose, and ears.

Matthew carried Emily up the hill to Jackson Avenue, over and through piles of strewn debris to reach 26th Street. There was a man driving a pickup truck on 26th Street with his wife and two children. The couple immediately stopped to help. They put Emily in the front seat of the cab. The rest of the family and Matthew climbed into the bed of the pickup truck. Emily was now talkative and in high spirits. She knew that she was going to be alright. When the driver got inside, Emily asked him if he really wanted her in the front seat where she would get blood on the seats.

When they reached Maiden Lane, there were many people in the street in front of the damaged hospital. The medical staff was using the street as a triage area, helping people coming out of the damaged hospital, as well as those who were coming to the hospital from the surrounding area for treatment.

A member of the medical staff placed Emily on a gurney. Before long, there would be no extra gurneys to be found. They started an I.V. right there on the street and then sent Emily over to Freeman Hospital for further treatment for her injuries. She was placed in the bed of another pickup truck with one injured woman for the 6-block ride to Freeman Hospital. Because she already had the initial I.V. in her arm, the emergency staff at Freeman Hospital were able to process her quickly.

Both Diane and Emily remembered the doctor who assisted Emily. The doctor said that he was retired and was just helping out in the emergency. He was small statured and had an extremely calming demeanor and conversation. From his action and calming voice, they both thought that he may have been a chaplain. Emily reassured her mother she knew everything was going to be alright. She smiled at all the workers as they walked past her that night. Emily did not feel any sense of urgency. She did not feel her injuries were any worse than any other person in the emergency room waiting area that day. She saw so many people who needed to be seen by the medical staff before she should be treated. By about 1 a.m., Emily would be taken by ambulance to the Labette County Hospital in Parsons, Kansas where she would spend the next 11 days going through further treatment.

Sometime after Emily returned home from the hospital, she was walking near their damaged home when a butterfly flew up to her and landed on her shoulder where the hand had touched her several weeks before while she lay on the office floor. She was standing in an area where all the trees had been toppled or destroyed. There was not much green vegetation anywhere nearby. She has had several occasions since then, in various locations, where a butterfly would land on her hand or her finger. It has happened over and over since then. A butterfly just flew to her finger and stayed there for a short period of time, then flew away. She could not recall anything like this happening before the storm. Emily has become acutely aware of butterflies since then. She says it seems like there are butterflies everywhere she looks now. To her the butterflies are reminders to her that angels were with her that day, and they are still here and have never gone away.

Emily does not feel adversely affected by the storm. Maggie still gets a little nervous when the winds on any given day begin to pick up noticeably. Emily continued to get a lot of support from her friends at school. She was told of the changes people had seen in her personality since her experience in the storm. Her outlook on life altered and she feels like she has been given the opportunity to change from the inside. She believes everything happens for a reason. Emily has had people tell her that the testimony of her experience in the storm has been such an inspiration to them. She would like to see an increased expansion of that help for others in her life. She prays God will hear her and reveal to her what she should do next.

When Diane and Emily think back to the precise events of that day, they wonder how the individual occurrences could have changed the outcome. What would be different if Emily had left the graduation ceremony with her older brother? That would have put one of the twins in the seat behind her father. Would they, without a car seat, have been able to survive the same forceful injury Emily experienced? Would they have made it home if Kenny had only put 5 dollars of gas in the tank instead of 20 dollars? Would he have been in the garage? How much farther down the road would they have been if the stoplight was green? Would the precious few seconds saved given them enough time to get safely into their house, or would they have still been trying to get the children out of the car in the garage? Would they have been ultimately safer in the missing garage than where they actually were in the Suburban? Their garage was gone. They realize there are numerous unanswerable questions which only lead to more questions. Diane resolves they were exactly where they were supposed to be, exactly when they were supposed to be there. It took Diane 3 or 4 days to process all the signs she saw around her that day. Diane said, "Now, more than ever, when you are in your darkest hour, God is there with His grace, love, and mercy."

Diane tells how settling it was that people came to help them. She did not have time to fear the uncertainty of everything around them. There were people around offering food, water, but, more importantly, their prayers and support. She was astonished at the multitude of people coming down their street over the next weeks or months to help. She realizes she did not know them, nor did they know her. They were just there, each a blessing to the other. She feels one of the ways to help with her healing is to thank those countless people for everything they did and to tell the story of how they were such a blessing to a total stranger.

As with all the other people who were interviewed for this project, Emily says she now acts differently. All recognize they have experienced and played a part in something very big. All look at things around them differently than they would have on May 21st. The material things they thought were important in their lives are somewhere between Joplin and Springfield or in a landfill. Either way, they are gone, and there is no reason to think they will ever come back. Diane says there were some memories from their home that would have been nice to keep, but their possessions are gone. At the time of the interview, they had not yet gone through the storage unit where their salvaged possessions were kept. Yet, Diane says she doesn't really miss them. She has what she needs. She has what she thinks is important now. You can see the joy. You can see the smiles.

Emily is not letting the injury keep her from doing anything, or even slowing her down. For her 13th birthday, she said she wanted to take tumbling lessons.

CHAPTER 17
HEALTH

"For He will give His angels [especial] charge over you to accompany and defend and preserve you in all your ways [of obedience and service]."—**Psalm 91:11 (AMPC)**

"Then an angel from heaven appeared to him to strengthen him."—**Luke 22:43 (NCV)**

Shirley was diving home on the central west side of Joplin, Missouri about 4:40 that Sunday afternoon. She, and her husband, Charles, were headed west on 20th Street near Virginia Avenue when they met the north wall of the funnel cloud. The sky had quickly turned black as the funnel passed less than 1 block south of their location. As the visibility outside dropped to almost nothing, Charles was forced to pull their Honda CR-X to the side of the road. Concerned about being rear-ended by another vehicle unable to see them in the rainy, windy darkness, he pulled as far over as he could to the right side of the street, just in front of Bethany Presbyterian Church. The church building would shield the tiny car from the full force of the winds from the north. The high winds knocked over the streetlight pole at the corner of 20th Street and Virginia Avenue and part of the light fixture crashed to the street, missing the front hood of the car by a few feet.

Shirley ducked down as all the car windows blew out. The right passenger's side mirror was jarred loose by the wind and debris and broke free from the door. It flew through the passenger window and struck Charles on the side of the head. Even as the high wind was destroying structures and vehicles all around, their tiny, 1,900-pound car, stayed put.

Charles decided to seek refuge from the driving rain and wind at the Walgreens store just to their left. He drove their damaged car around to the side of the store to get protection from the north wind. There was already a pickup truck parked under the roof of the pharmacy drive-thru lane by the time they pulled in. He pulled next to the vehicle and sat in the car. Shirley noticed a few people standing around. The rain was pouring down.

Shirley, suffering from asthma, was sitting in the car, trying desperately to catch her breath. She was shivering from the cold rain that was blowing through the missing windows. Charles later said he was worried that his wife would not survive the asthma attack. As she sat in the car, a man wearing a large, oversize, dry, white shirt approached her. He stood next to the car door and spoke with her, confirming that she was having a difficult time trying to breathe. She had not said anything to him to indicate her breathing difficulties. She agreed with him and told him of her asthma. He took her by the hand, opened the car door for her, and walked around the front of the pickup truck with her. They stood between the pickup truck and the glass drive-thru pharmacy window of the store. She doesn't recall what he said, if anything, but he held her hands as she closed her eyes and took a few deep breaths.

After just a brief moment, she opened her eyes and noticed she was standing alone. He was gone. There was no one around her. Her breathing rate had returned to normal and the chill from the rain had stopped. As she looked at her arms and hands, she saw there were no scratches or injuries from the broken glass.

When pressed to describe the man, Shirley said she first noticed him walking toward her in the midst of the storm activity. From where she sat low in the car, she was able to estimate his age as mid-30s. He had brown, shoulder-length hair. She recalls his oversize shirt was remarkably clean and white. It had long sleeves. There was not a collar visible on the shirt that reached just below his knees. She also observed that the shirt was dry, even while the rain was pouring down just beyond the protection of the awning.

Shirley noted that the characteristics of dry and clean, were inconsistent with the immediate surroundings. Everything around had been saturated by the driving rain and was covered with the slurry mix consisting of mud, insulation, glass, wood, and other various components, forming a "brown yuck," similar to a riverbank after a season of flooding. She saw nothing around her that was either clean or dry, much less both, except for his shirt.

❖ ❖ ❖

When Ken and his wife, Katherine, arrived at church for the 5 p.m. service that Sunday, the weather outside seemed perfectly normal. It was just a hot, humid day. Storm watches and warnings had been issued earlier in the day, but nothing seemed out of the ordinary. Two men from the church who served as hall monitors were stationed to keep an eye on the weather, just in case things changed. One of the church members was a part-time police officer in Duquesne, Missouri and was monitoring the storm's progress on his police radio. At one point, he came into the service and reported St. John's Hospital had been hit by the storm. The church, located near Joplin High School, did not have a designated "safe room," but there was a brick-walled interior hallway thought to be the safest place in the building.

Once the people in the congregation were notified of the approaching storm, nearly everyone walked calmly into the hallway to ride it out. There were a few people who sought shelter in a library on the other side of the wall. As a hall monitor, Ken was the last person to retreat to the hallway. The storm reached the church minutes after they learned about the hospital. Katherine squatted down and grabbed hold of a nearby cabinet. When the cabinet started dancing around, she went with it.

As soon as Ken stepped into the hallway, the lights went out. The sky had grown darker, making it very difficult to see inside the interior hallway. He had to feel his way down the hall to reach the people who had gone ahead of him. The circumstances seemed surreal, almost like a dream, as he reached a partition wall halfway down the hallway. There was some indecision about what to do or where to go next. Ken could hear the wind and the debris hitting the outside of the building. While he paused, a blast of debris flew through the room from behind Ken, striking him in the head. Then a piece of wooden 2x4 struck him on the side of the head, followed immediately by a large blast of wind from behind him. "I went flying without my airplane," Ken later said. He landed about 10 feet down the hall from where he was standing initially. He looked up to see the roof had come off the church building.

When the storm had passed, everything that had surrounding them just 5 minutes earlier now was reduced to a large pile of twisted, shattered rubble. Katherine ended up under the piles of debris. She could see light near the end of the hallway after the storm had passed. She assumed the emergency lights had kicked on. She did not realize the light was from the open sky. She did not hear any sounds from any of the other people for a few minutes after the wind, hail, and rain stopped. She was laying in a pool of water and ice when she was pulled from the debris. There was an overturned car on top of the debris pile just a few yards away.

Both Ken and Katherine felt as if they had been "sandblasted." They had debris embedded into their ears, noses, eyes, mouths, skin, scalps, hair, and clothes. They removed grit and debris for several weeks afterward.

Ken was taking a blood thinner. When that flying board struck Ken in the head with such a hard blow, it caused him to bleed externally. Normally, for a person on a blood thinner, even the smallest of cuts is cause for concern as it diminishes the body's ability to clot the blood. Any internal bleeding could be prolonged and have drastic results before the bleeding would stop. Though Ken was bleeding from the injury, he was able to get the bleeding stopped. It was notable that Ken's cut stopped bleeding on its own in mere minutes and that there was not a brain bleed from the hard blow to the side of his head.

Katherine says that, "Only by the grace of God had anybody made it out of the church building alive." Ken believes God must have some big plans for both of them because he said, "We feel extremely blessed to be alive today as there were many opportunities for us not to be."

CHAPTER 18
HERE, THEN GONE

"Cornelius answered, 'Four days ago I was praying at home. It was at this same time, three o'clock in the afternoon. Suddenly, a man dressed in radiant clothes stood in front of me.'"—**Acts 10:30 (GW)**

"And while they were perplexed and wondering what to do about this, behold, two men in dazzling raiment suddenly stood beside them."—**Luke 24:4 (AMPC)**

Sunday, May 22, 2011, appeared to be a normal, hot, late spring day. Melvin and Tina had decided to leave their large lab mix dog inside because of the heat. Their sons, Melvin, 12, and Michael, 8, were playing outside their home just east of St. Mary's Church. They knew of the storm warnings but did not notice anything unusual or threatening. The warning sirens sounded briefly and then stopped when the storm was believed to be headed farther north.

Melvin and Tina were on their east-facing front porch watching the rain, believing any danger was far away. Then the second storm warning siren started and then stopped. Unknown to them, the siren, positioned just west of them stopped, not because it was "all clear," but because the power to the siren was lost due to the high winds and debris from the storm. Melvin came inside to double check the weather on the local programming to find out why the sirens were erratic. Their boys ran inside to tell their father that the sky had gotten very dark, very fast. Tina stepped off the porch to look back to the west and saw a wall of horizontal rain headed directly toward them. She yelled for everybody to get into the basement. Melvin told the boys to get their shoes on and grab the cat from the back of the living room chair on their way through to the basement. Tina would be right behind them as soon as she could get the dog downstairs.

The power went out as the family ran through the dining room. As they got through the kitchen and reached the top of the basement stairs, the windows in the house started breaking. By now, it was nearly as dark as night. Melvin and the boys could not see anything when they reached the bottom of the stairs. They headed, without any hesitation, to the 6 by 6-foot square coal room in the southeast corner of the basement, near the front of the house. Tina had asked Melvin before if they would be safe in the coal room in case there was a tornado. He assured her that it would withstand an F4 tornado, but he knew he could never guarantee its strength against an F5. That strength was just about to be tested. Melvin and the boys made it across the dark basement and into the coal room in just a few seconds and he had them get under a table in the small room, then he went back toward the stairs to help Tina. She was still trying to get the dog into the basement. There was so much commotion that the dog would not go down the stairs—there just was not enough time. Leaving the dog upstairs, both Melvin and Tina made it back down to the coal room and huddled around their boys under the table.

The noise was as piercing as a jet engine and constant. Melvin was concerned the cover of the coal chute, just above his head, was going to be pulled off by the force of the wind. In the darkness of the room, Melvin began to recite part of Psalm 23, "... *Though I walk through the valley of the shadow of death, I will fear no evil, for You are with me...*" and Tina and the boys joined in, as the storm roared around them. Though it was dark in the tiny coal room, Melvin could see the silhouette of a set of wings that rose up and unfolded around the four of them as they huddled together. The presence brought a feeling of safety and peace that stayed with him through the duration of the storm.

The family lingered together beneath the table for a few minutes after the wind and hail in the storm had passed. The rain still poured. In the stillness, they heard three sharp knocks at the front door. Melvin, a 12-year veteran of the United States Marine Corps, was certain that search and rescue teams would be canvassing the area. He told his family to stay put in the basement and made his way to the stairs. When he got to the top of the stairs, the dog, unhurt, was standing there waiting for him. It was covered in dirty insulation and looked like a polar bear. He walked past the dog into the kitchen and saw daylight when he looked up. There was debris in the kitchen, mostly glass, sheetrock, and insulation, but he could get through that room without too much difficulty; he was telling himself that the damage was minimal. The storm had not completely cleared up. It was still raining with dusk-like lighting.

As he walked through the kitchen and into the dining room, he noticed there were large sections of the ceiling sheetrock missing. Rain was coming through the openings and dripping throughout the room. In the midst of it all was a middle-aged man standing next to the dining room table in the center of the room. He was wearing blue jeans, a white shirt, and a white baseball cap. He addressed Melvin by name asking, "Melvin, are you and your family alright?" Melvin answered, "Yes, we're fine." The man said, "OK, I've got to go," then turned around and headed toward the front room, just behind him.

Melvin noticed several peculiarities about the stranger in the baseball cap. For search and rescue efforts, he got there very quickly; only a few minutes after the storm had slammed into the house. It also seemed unusual that this man, whom he had never seen before or afterward, called Melvin by name. Also, the man's clothes were clean and dry, this while standing in a room that had no roof and only part of a ceiling, in the middle of a pouring rainstorm. Melvin recognized the clean dry clothes on the man did not correlate with the insulation and debris-covered dog in the next room or the pouring rain that had not stopped since the storm started. Melvin followed 5 to 6 feet behind the man as he walked into the front living room. "That was the last I saw of him," Melvin said. When he turned the corner into the front room, he was alone. As quickly as the stranger had come, he had gone.

Melvin, trying to reason to himself what just happened, walked over to the parlor/office just off the front room to see if the man had possibly gone out that way. One of the French doors into the office was ripped off the hinges and was sticking through the front window. There was only a small, 10-inch wide opening next to the door, not enough for anybody to squeeze through.

Melvin opened the front door. There was debris stacked from floor to ceiling on the front porch, mostly commercial roofing and venting. There was no way to get outside through the front door. He walked to the back door to see if there was any exit available there. When he opened the back door, he saw the ceiling of the back porch had collapsed against the back door and blocked any exit there as well. There was no way in or out.

It took Melvin and Tina nearly 30 minutes to kick a hole in the roof that had fallen down to block the back door, just to get out of the house. Melvin did not realize the scope of the damage until he had gotten outside. The roof was gone, not even a remnant of it remaining on their lawn. The ceiling in much of the house had fallen already. What remained was held in place by wires and flanges of their ceiling fans, only to fall when those fixtures were removed.

Tina added, "The first gust of wind was the angels and the second was the storm."

Tina has always referred to an F5 tornado as the "Hand of

God." Melvin believes that more now than ever. The outpouring of people from all over—not just Joplin or the surrounding communities, but from much further distances—who came to give selflessly, inspired Melvin and lifted his spirits. He said there was a car with Pennsylvania license plates that pulled up in front of his house about 1 p.m. on Monday to offer help; only 18 hours after the storm hit Joplin. The family must have left Pennsylvania without hesitation and drove through the night to get there. Children rode throughout their neighborhoods handing out bottles of cold water mixed with Kool-Aid, from baskets fastened to their bicycles. Churches came together and did what they are supposed to do. They did not separate themselves by denomination. They just all helped each person as they could.

◆ ◆ ◆

Mary spent part of that Sunday working in her mother's shop at Northpark Mall in Joplin, Missouri. A number of customers in the store had already cleared out, nothing unusual for a Sunday afternoon. As Mary was getting ready to leave, one of the security guards passed by and informed her the storm sirens were sounding. Even though they spoke of how it was probably nothing to worry about, he asked Mary to be careful as she packed up to head home.

Mary was looking forward to getting to her home near Irving Elementary School. She had just had countertops installed in her newly remodeled kitchen the day before. It seemed like a good time to relax and bake some cookies.

As she walked out of the mall, Mary looked at the sky around her. It was not raining, and the clouds did not appear abnormal. She drove south on Range Line Road, noticing the sky was starting to grow dark. She did not suspect anything unusual, just a normal thunderstorm. As Mary sat at the intersection of 17th Street and Range Line Road, waiting for the stoplight to turn green, all at once it, and every light around, went dark. Nearby, a man ran out of the AT&T store on the corner, jumped into his car, and sped out of the parking lot. She wondered why he was in such a hurry.

Meanwhile, another woman, Sheryl, and her daughters, Amanda and Laura, had just left Laura's Joplin High School graduation ceremony at Missouri Southern State University. Warning sirens sounded as people discussed the approaching storm and reasoned that it would probably never make it to Joplin. The sky overhead did not look that unusual. Sheryl did not feel an extraordinary sense of urgency or panic at the time. She drove south on Duquesne Road to 20th Street and planned on taking 20th Street to Connecticut Avenue, then turn south toward her home. She stopped momentarily at the traffic signal on 20th Street facing west at Range Line Road. As she and her daughters waited on the light, the dark gray sky to the west was eerily highlighted by a much lighter sky to the north and south. Three cars in front of and behind them made U-turns and headed back to the east. For a brief moment, as they sat in their blue Mercury Villager, the sun popped out from behind the clouds. They commented on the darker clouds directly ahead of them to the west, believing it was just very heavy rain. The storm sirens stopped and they believed they would be home before the storm would actually reach them.

Mary drove through the intersection at 17th Street and turned west on 20th Street just a block or so behind Sheryl. The sky had gotten considerably darker by now. Because of all the large trees in the neighborhoods, she was not able to see any cloud rotation, debris, or other telltale signs of an approaching tornado. The rain had picked up significantly as she headed west. The light sprinkle at Range Line Road quickly transitioned into moderate hail, and then into a heavy downpour in a matter of about 10 blocks. She continued driving toward Main Street, unaware that she was headed directly into the storm. The wind began to blow much harder and hail began to pound her car— she was concerned her car was going to get damaged. The storm had just ravaged Joplin High School and was moving east down 20th Street, destroying everything in its path. She would come face to face with the full fury of the storm in just a matter of moments.

As Sheryl neared Delaware Avenue, visibility was reduced to zero. She briefly caught a glimpse of Delaware Avenue to her right through the heavy rain, so she turned north and drove about a block. Her visibility improved slightly, and she began to see flying debris. Sheryl had a sense that she was only to drive a short distance on Delaware Avenue before she should stop her van. Even amid the impending storm, Sheryl felt a sense of peace envelope her and her daughters.

Visibility was reduced to about 50 feet. Mary could not see anything beyond the few rain-obscured cars ahead of her. As she waited just short of the intersection of Delaware Avenue and 20th Street, for a brief moment the intensity of the rain and the hail let up just a little bit. The thought of an actual tornado was still not a consideration for Mary. She decided to try to take a detour from the traffic jam in front of her and turned north on Delaware Avenue. No sooner had she turned on Delaware Avenue to get freed from the traffic jam on 20th Street, she was stopped again. Nobody was moving. There was no way to get past Sheryl's van and an SUV that were parked on the street there. Again, Mary came to a complete stop on Delaware Avenue, only a few yards from 20th Street.

Mary was still unaware of the presence of the storm bearing down on them from the west. With nowhere to go and unable to move forward, Mary came to the realization she was stuck and put the gearshift of her Ford Focus into park. In that same moment, all the windows of her car blew out. She looked back over her shoulder and saw the dark clouds of the tornado rolling in. It was not more than a block or two away. For the first time, she was able to physically see the tornado. She could see through the dense curtain of rain the bright blue flashes of light as the transformers on the nearby electric poles blew out. Mary remembered some of the tornado safety steps and precautions, the "dos and don'ts" necessary for survival in the presence of a tornado, she had heard repeated many times. She knew that being inside a car was not a good place to be. The car might not stay firmly on the ground in high winds. It could be picked up and rolled or tossed for great distances. The metal panels of the roof and doors would offer little to no protection from the flying debris carried in a tornado. She knew she had to get down as close to the ground as possible. If there was a ditch available, that would be a better place to be. She needed to get out of the car quickly. There were a few seconds left before it would be too late, if it wasn't already.

Mary unlatched her seat belt to allow her to get out of the car. As soon as she unfastened her seat belt, the driver's door was violently ripped open. She doesn't know if it had been forced open by an impact of flying debris or if the force of the wind grabbed hold of it. The interior panel of the door and all the internal parts of the door were blown away, leaving just the skeleton frame and the exterior door panel attached.

Before Mary could get out of the mangled shell of the car, the wind whipped it around with her still inside. She became separated from the car very quickly after that. She ended up on the ground near the curb on the west side of Delaware Avenue, close to the corner of 20th Street. There was no ditch to get into. She struggled to crawl to the curb about 10 feet away from where she lay in the middle of the street. Once separated from the car, she was pounded by the debris—broken sheet rock, chunks of asphalt shingles, splintered lumber, and other sizable objects. She felt several times as if there was a large hand holding her down. She could feel herself being lifted up off the ground by the wind, and then the firm hand would push her back down to the ground. She felt the hand several times before she had dragged herself to the curb.

As Mary was battered by debris, she thought she was not going to be able to last long in the storm. She saw flashes of intense, bright light, even through her closed eyelids and imagined it was some of the remaining electrical transformers flashing as they blew apart. The noise she heard was intense, like a freight train but much, much louder.

Inside Sheryl's van, her daughters took cover. Laura crouching low on the floor of the front seat, covering her head with a large, heavy handbag. Amanda ducking behind Sheryl as the windows around them began to spider and crack, before blowing out completely. In the midst of all this, their mother wedged herself over the console between the front seats, trying to protect her daughters. During the front half of the storm, their van stayed fairly stationary. Yet, as the van was buffeted by wind and debris, they prayed for protection and deliverance, and felt a strong sense of God's presence.

With the eye of the storm passed, the back half brought a new round of debris, freezing rain, and hail. This half of the storm was much more intense. The battered van was picked up and tossed back and forth before coming to rest just off the roadway on a large detached section of roof blown from a house.

Hoping someone would see her, Mary reached her hand to the sky as she lay on the ground during the storm. Surely, someone would come to her aid; but it was a futile effort. The first thing to die down was the wind, the worst of the hail and rain following, bringing a welcome brightening to the sky. But still, as Mary lay face down next to the curb, covered in debris except for her hands and feet, the rain continued on; fairly heavy, but thankfully mixed with almost no hail.

As soon as Mary was able to move her hands and feet, a

gentleman arrived to help her. She did not see where he came from as he walked to where she lay. She thought at first that he may have walked out from the house on the east side of the street, but it was gone except for a couple of partial walls. When she looked around, she saw all the buildings nearby were nearly leveled. There was nothing else around her except piles of debris —lots and lots of debris.

The man had red hair and freckles. He looked like he was in his mid to late 20s and wearing sneakers, jeans, a white T-shirt, and a red jacket. Mary was covered from head to toe with the same debris slurry that coated everything around her, yet this man and his clothes were completely clean. She wondered where he came from or where he was during the storm, and how he managed to stay dry as he stood next to her in the rain. Was he in the basement of one of the demolished homes nearby? She noted he had no marks or even a stain on his clothing. He had no sign of debris in his hair or even on his jacket. His T-shirt looked brand new.

"Are you alright," he asked, then helped to free her from the debris and stood her to her feet.

As Mary was able to stand, she looked around at the barren landscape. All the buildings that surrounded her moments before were gone. The glassless shell of her car ended up not too far from where she lay. The wind had scooted the car, left in park, about 100 feet north, near the corner of 19th Street and Delaware Avenue. It came to rest on top of a pile of debris, about 6 feet off the ground. The car, with the driver's door still peeled back, acted like a funnel for the debris. There were boards, shingles, and all kinds of storm junk that filled much of the car's interior. There were 2x4s piercing the roof over the driver's seat, extending through the middle of the seat. Had Mary not gotten out of the car when she did, she would most likely have ended up in much worse shape. The tread on her fairly new tires had been ground off, exposing some of the steel belts within. The mid-size SUV that had been stopped in front of her car just before the force of the storm hit had come to rest upside down, partially up against the skeleton of a tree on the east side of Delaware Avenue, between 19th and 20th Streets.

The kind man in the red jacket assured Mary she was going to be alright, and that he would stay with her and get her to where she needed to be. She told him she needed to get her purse and backpack from her car that was sitting on top of a debris pile just a short distance away. She was unable to climb the pile to get her things out, but the gentleman disappeared around the other side of the car and quickly came back with both the backpack and purse in his hands. He stood next to Mary as she got her phone out of her purse to call her mother. She was able to let her mother know that she had been in a tornado, and was alright. Shortly after, Mary's phone went dead.

The man then went to help Sheryl and her daughters out of their mangled van. In a calm, soft-spoken voice, he assured Sheryl that the fallen power lines draped over the van were not live. Sheryl felt a strong sense of calmness, peace, and trust when the young man approached the van. She noticed, as Mary had, that the appearance of this man was remarkable. In contrast with the gray, filthy, wet clothes of everybody else, his clothes were completely clean and seemed dry. He told Sheryl, "Do not be afraid. I am going to get you out of here." Amanda and Laura were able to push the battered van door with their feet while he pulled it open from the outside. As he took each one of them by the hand, helping them out of the van, they knew they were going to be alright.

Other people began to move around in and amid the wreckage piled in the streets and yards nearby. The gentleman with the red jacket remained with Mary the entire time. They decided they should walk toward Walgreen's on 20th and Main Streets, about a mile and a half to the west. As Sheryl and Laura walked along, Mary, Amanda, and the gentleman followed just behind them. There was a strong smell from the debris as well as the odor of natural gas from the wreckage. They were concerned about the possibility of a fire or explosion from a spark with the natural gas fumes that filled the air. Sheryl suggested they pick up the pace to get past the gas fumes. Mary knew she was hurt and probably needed to get to the hospital, but she did not know how extensive her injuries were. She had a cut on the left side of her face and the tip of one finger was nearly severed. As they began to jog past the natural gas-filled area, the man spoke in a direct, authoritative tone, "Stop! Her injuries..." Sheryl thought that he was referring to the cuts on Mary's face. Neither Mary, Sheryl, nor her daughters were aware of any of Mary's further injuries.

The rain had stopped by the time they reached Connecticut Avenue, but an abundance of runoff was flowing along 20th Street. More people were filling the streets. The traffic on Connecticut Avenue was already backing up. Some people were looking for family members or friends, while others were just looking. A few vehicles approached from 24th Street, a few blocks south. Mary flagged down a man in the first vehicle she saw to see if she could get a ride to the hospital. He was unable to help her. The second car had a young man and woman with some children. They had no room for another passenger.

Mary was unaware that casualties lay around her as she walked along 20th Street. The only thing that kept her from seeing and dwelling on the surrounding carnage was her ability to stay focused on where she needed to go. The gentleman remained beside her the entire time. It was very comforting to have him by her side. It allowed her to take her mind off all the negative things surrounding her. There was peace amidst the chaos for Mary as she was comforted by the gentleman helping her and watching over her. He never wavered from his first statement that he would stay with her and help get her to where she needed.

A third car carried a woman and her husband. Mary talked with Jeff, the driver, but she could see the gentleman in the red jacket standing next to her out of the corner of her eye. Sheryl and her daughters were standing nearby as she spoke. Jeff offered to take her to the hospital and seated Mary in the back seat of the car. Mary would not see the young man again.

The couple in the car appeared to be in their 40s. Jeff and his wife, Tawn, were in the neighborhood because they believed his daughter might be at her mother's house near 20th Street and Delaware Avenue for a post-graduation party. Tawn stayed with Mary in the car as Jeff ran down the street to check on his daughter and her mother. Tawn wrapped Mary in a blanket to keep her warm. Mary had started to chill from cold rain and her injuries. Tawn talked with Mary to get some information from her, just in case it would be needed at the hospital, and used Mary's cell phone to call Mary's mother to let her know she was safe and where they would be taking her. Jeff returned to the car, unsuccessful at finding his daughter and her mother. They decided to take Mary on to the hospital due to the seriousness of her injuries. They would come back afterwards to search for the pair.

As Jeff and Tawn left with Mary, the young gentleman asked Sheryl, "Are you going to be alright?" Sheryl answered, "Yes," and he repeated the question. She again gave the same answer. "Then I am going on," he said. As she walked south on Connecticut Avenue, the last time she saw the gentleman, he was walking west on 20th Street.

Jeff drove west on 20th Street toward Main Street. The street was covered with debris, making driving was difficult. Their car was stopped by an off-duty fireman clearing the roadway on 20th Street near the ravaged shell of Joplin High School. Jeff described Mary's visible head injury to the firefighter, who, after climbing in the back seat of the car to check her injuries himself, agreed she needed to get to the hospital quickly. They had planned on going to St. John's Hospital, but were unable to get through and drove to Freeman Hospital instead.

Once they got to the hospital, Mary began to feel intense pain in her back. As Tawn walked into the crowded emergency waiting room with Mary, she saw that every seat was taken. Tawn noticed an unused wheelchair immediately in front of her and helped Mary to sit down. A nurse in the crowded emergency room examined Mary to see if she could find the cause of her back pain. To their shock, Mary had a nearly 10-inch-long piece of splintered board buried inside her back. They placed a neck brace on her and moved her near the front of the line at the check-in desk. Due to the large number of wounded people, Mary would wait for several hours in the wheelchair before she could be more closely evaluated.

The hospital was a depiction of controlled chaos as Mary waited for treatment. There was a calm stillness after the storm as people recalled the details of their experiences. People were being brought into the emergency room in pickup trucks, on four-wheelers, and on doors and other makeshift gurneys, some comprised of broomsticks with sheets. People would code right in front of them, and the nurses and doctors would work feverishly to resuscitate them right where they were. There were so many people waiting to receive treatment. Mary's father arrived at the emergency room about 2 hours later and she saw him and called out his name as he passed by. He turned toward Mary and just stared at her as she was unrecognizable to him. Eighty percent of her body was bruised and she was covered in debris.

Mary was released from the hospital June 13th. Sheryl, who walked with her that day, called Mary and asked her about the gentleman walking with them. The details surrounding the gentleman were remarkable—his clothes clean and his demeanor, presence, and voice extremely calming and comforting. There was no noticeable anxiety or excitement in his tone. There was a strong sense of assuring peace that accompanied him. Mary sensed and acknowledged the same presence. They could not offer any explanation. Sheryl told her that she believed the man was an angel sent from God. Mary finds it much easier to tell her story to older people who waste no time in telling Mary that her freckle-faced friend was an angel. Some people tell her they are happy to meet a storm survivor. Others tell of their joy of meeting someone who has met an angel.

Mary knows the gentleman was there to provide peace and guidance to her in a moment of crisis. He kept his promise to get her to where she needed to be. She knows that, had she stayed in the car, her life may have ended that day. About a week after the storm, Mary's mother broke the news to Mary that Mary's home was also destroyed in the storm. The outcome for Mary may have been worse had she made it home. The worst part of damage to her home was her living room and bedroom. The basement ended up being barricaded by debris, which would have trapped her in a subterranean room filled with gas from a leaking main.

Since the storm, Mary has taken serious introspection into her life before the storm compared to after. Before the storm, her life was chaotic. She struggled daily and took things for granted. Today, she is able to roll with things and it is easier to cope with the frustrations of everyday life. She believes there is a reason for everything. She breathes in the small things and realizes that God has a bigger and better plan for her.

◆ ◆ ◆

I t was about 5:30 p.m. when Erin left her home in Webb City, Missouri to go to her church near Joplin High School for the Sunday evening service. She was just turning west on 20th

Street from Range Line Road when she received a phone call from her daughter. Erin's daughter was watching a movie with some friends at the Northstar Movie Theater near Northpark Mall when management stopped the movie and directed everyone to move toward the front lobby. The girl made a second call to her mother and told her to turn around and go back home. Erin assured her daughter that she was not too far and should be able to get to the church safely.

Just after Erin turned from Range Line Road, the rain intensified. She heard a weather report of 60-mile-per-hour winds and pea-sized hail, but never considered that a tornado was nearby. The sky rapidly changed and became a huge black wall of darkness in front of her. She was not able to see anything through the dense black cloud. Debris began to blow across the street in front of her car. It worsened as she drove farther away from Range Line Road. On the phone again with her daughter, she decided to concentrate more on navigating through the deteriorating weather conditions and hung up. As she headed west, Erin was praying for direction and protection from danger. She thought about turning on Murphy Boulevard, but felt a strong sense in her spirit that she should continue going west on 20th Street, right into the rapidly approaching front face of the storm. Erin felt directed in her spirit to turn on Delaware Avenue and to pull in behind a van that had already stopped there.

The weather had become next to impossible to contend with. Hail, debris, and heavy rain reduced visibility to about 40 feet. She continued to pray to God for guidance, safety, and protection. She turned north on Delaware Avenue and pulled her Saturn behind a blue van and next to a small, light-colored car stopped in the roadway. There was another car in the group as well, but details were difficult to make out well as the rain and wind had become intense. The light-colored car was just 10 to 15 feet ahead of Erin on the left side. Erin's Saturn had come to a stop only about 10 feet from the corner of 20th Street and

Delaware Avenue, she would have to wait until the rain and wind stopped before she could drive.

Within a few seconds of parking her car, the windows and sunroof shattered. Erin immediately turned on her emergency flashers and started honking the horn. She put her hands up to shield her head and face from all the debris flying through the car. She put her head down on the passenger seat in an attempt to avoid the debris pummeling her vehicle. As she was trying to protect herself, the wind picked the car up off the ground briefly and slammed it back down to the pavement. She did not lose consciousness, but was hit very hard on the head by debris that flew into the car. Erin managed to grab hold of a large, jagged piece of plywood to shield herself. The intense wind-driven rain and debris seemed to last forever.

The small car next to her came to rest on top of a large pile of debris near the corner of 19th Street and Delaware Avenue. (NOTE: If this story sounds like you have heard it before, it is because you have. The light-colored car Erin describes IS THE SAME CAR occupied by Mary in the story just prior to this one. Erin and Mary had ended up only about 8 to 10 feet apart in cars parked next to each other as the storm hit.)

The blue van that was stopped in front of Erin's Saturn ended up coming to rest about 20 yards down the street. The other vehicle in the immediate group ended upside down against a tree in the yard to Erin's right. Erin's car had come to rest in the yard just about 10 feet east from where she first started.

After Erin's car came to a stop and the wind stilled, a very tall gentleman arrived beside her now windowless car. She had no idea where he came from. There were not many structures left standing around them. The gentleman asked Erin if she was alright. He said his name was Joshua. Erin assured him she was alright and not hurt badly. As he was standing next to her car, the hail began to fall. Joshua asked if he could get inside the car to get out of the pounding hail. He climbed into the back seat where he sat quietly. He did not say much at all as Erin sat in the debris-filled front seat, still praying out loud to God. While they were both sitting there, a woman walked up to the driver's side door. She had a large cut on her forehead and was bleeding profusely. She asked Erin if she could get a ride to the hospital. Erin agreed that, assuming her car was still drivable, she would take the woman to the hospital as soon as the hail stopped. The woman agreed and climbed into the back next to Joshua. After welcoming the injured woman into her car, Erin came to the realization that she had been spared from this terrible tornado. All three of them sat there in the hail pummeled car for almost 20 minutes, until 6:10 p.m. Erin had cuts and bruises all over her left side. She was cold and wet from the rain that poured down on them immediately before, during, and after the storm.

After the hail had almost stopped, the woman sitting in the back seat, felt she was becoming nauseous. Erin feared the woman was about to go into shock. She would have to do something to help her very soon.

Erin was unable to get her driver's door open because of some power lines that had fallen over her side of the car. Joshua, after getting out of the back seat of the car, reached up and pulled the dead power lines from the top of the car, and helped Erin out. He was wearing a red and yellow plaid western-style shirt, regular "Wrangler-style" blue jeans with a bandana in the back pocket, and cowboy boots. He was young in appearance, maybe 25 years old. His face was clean shaven, reminding Erin of a good old country boy. His clothes were not wet or dirty. He seemed extraordinarily tall in stature. Even after riding out the storm in a glassless car with heavy hail and pouring rain, he was still clean, and his clothes appeared to be completely dry.

The gentleman assured Erin repeatedly that everything was going to be alright during the brief time he was there with her. He told her they were going to make it through this. Erin remembers that while Joshua was standing there, she could feel God's grace and mercy around her. A strong sense of peace washed over her as he stood there and that incredible, strong sense of encouraging peace that enveloped her stayed with her for the rest of that day.

Unable to drive, Erin, Joshua, and the woman walked together back to 20th Street just a few yards behind her car and then west toward Connecticut Avenue. Erin was carrying her purse and Bible as they walked along. They had not gotten very far down 20th Street when Erin saw a white van approaching. They flagged it down and it pulled up beside them. Erin asked the driver if he could take the woman to the hospital and the driver agreed. Erin and Joshua helped the young woman get into the back of the van. With the woman situated, Erin went to close the door and noticed Joshua standing beside her. As soon as the door closed, Erin turned around and Joshua was nowhere to be found.

Erin looked around and could see only the foundations and slabs of concrete where the homes nearby once stood. Debris was strewn everywhere. The streets were littered with vehicles that had been beaten and battered.

She began walking west toward Main Street. She was soon joined by two teenagers; the girl was wrapped in a large blanket. As they walked along 20th Street, there was another van that stopped to help them. This time, Erin got into the van with the two teens. As she sat on layers of broken glass riding in the back seat, Erin began to feel nauseous and worried that she too would go into shock. The driver stopped the van when he reached Wisconsin Avenue, near the destroyed Dillons grocery store, to look for his two daughters who had been at his sister's house in the neighborhood. The two teenagers got out of the van and went on their way. Erin became more nauseous because of a strong smell of natural gas in the air and decided to get out and walk along by herself. Still carrying her purse and Bible, she finally made it to her damaged church near the high school.

Erin's daughter had come to the church a short time before to look for Erin. Not finding her there, she went on to the hospital to search for her. They were reunited about 4 hours later, and eventually made it to their home in Webb City around 11 p.m.

Erin did not register at the time the significance of the name of Joshua. Joshua in the Old Testament means, "God is my salvation." The name "Joshua" in the Old Testament is the original Hebrew form of the Greek name "Jesus" in the New Testament.

Erin has received encouragement from some of the people who hear her recounting of what happened that day. She believes God had His angels all over the city of Joplin on the day of the storm. She shares with many the sense of peace that came upon her in the midst of chaos and destruction. Erin believes that she has been able to offer encouragement to other survivors by talking to them about her experience. They could realize there was more to this storm than just high wind, hail, destruction, and debris. There was a sense of peace and calm for those people as well. Sharing the story of her deliverance from the storm over and over, Erin believes it has helped in the healing process. Erin takes comfort in knowing she is the subject according to Hebrews 1:14, *"Are they not all ministering spirits sent forth to minister for those who will inherit salvation?"* She knows there is a reason for everything that happens.

Erin is continuing to put the negative aspects of the storm behind her. She, as many in Joplin have experienced, suffered a little setback when the sirens sounded in the city the next day. There was some anxiety of losing her car temporarily; she was able to get assistance from some friends in church to get her car replaced. Erin is keenly aware God has had His Hand on her every step of the way: financially, physically, emotionally, and spiritually. She has felt His peace and comfort in all the seemingly unexpected things that have come her way. Erin feels she has been given an opportunity to minister to people who suffered personally from the storm. She has a pretty good idea what they are going through. She was there.

◆ ◆ ◆

Cecil and 4 co-workers were waiting on 14 customers who had come into the store near Range Line Road and 20th Street that Sunday afternoon. One of the employees had started their first day of work just hours earlier. They heard the storm warning sirens sound but didn't react as they had heard too many before without any serious consequence.

Cecil's employer commented that the sky was quickly growing dark and looking less like a hot, late spring afternoon. She told Cecil they needed to turn on the lights on the business sign outside. Cecil walked outside to make sure the lights actually came on and gave his boss a "thumbs up" when the sign was lit. While Cecil was still outside the store, he was drenched by a single curtain of rain that blew across the parking lot. The storm warning sirens were still sounding as they had been doing so for about 5 minutes. Until then, Cecil was unaware that a massive storm was chewing its way through the city; when he looked west down 20th Street, he saw the storm, cloaked in a rain curtain, and bearing down on them. It was only about 6 blocks away and closing fast. The sky had become almost pitch black with an eerie green cast.

Cecil ran back inside the store, just as he made it through the front door, the lights flickered and then went dark. The employees quickly directed the customers to the restrooms at the back of the store. They believed the compact restrooms would offer the best protection. The restrooms and storage room were toward the outer, west wall and southwest corner of the building. After helping the customers to split up into the restrooms, Cecil, 17, and three other teens who were there without family members, sought shelter in the storage room next to the restrooms. The first destructive blast pounded the store less than 30 seconds after Cecil initially saw the approaching storm.

"The intense, scary, roaring noise was almost demonic," Cecil said. "It sounded like a very deep growl. It was louder than a large number of freight trains. I imagine it was louder than standing behind a jet."

As Cecil and the teenagers in the storage room were crouching down, the walls of the room began to shake. The noise and the wind seemed like it was going on forever. Debris was flying inside the store. It was comparable to an earthquake, but then briefly stopped and became strangely silent as the eye of the storm passed overhead. As quickly as the wind and the incredible noise ceased, it started back up again. The rumbling, roaring, and shaking resumed. The roof peeled back, rain poured in and hail pounded them.

A Lincoln Navigator that had been parked just beyond the outside wall of the storage room was blown into the outer wall, sending a large crack down the wall behind them. Even with the large crack in the outside wall of the storage room present, the SUV provided enough support to keep the wall from collapsing— when the vehicle was later removed, the walls collapsed.

As the teens prayed out loudly, they could hear a family in the adjacent restroom singing Gospel hymns, praying, and praising God above the intense noise of the storm.

As soon as the storm passed, Cecil was able to step safely out of the storage room and toward the restrooms. He was only able to make it a few feet from the doorway before he reached piles of debris that blocked his way. The ceiling had fallen, and large parts of the roof had collapsed into the store. The sky to the east was still very dark as the storm headed out of the city to points east. Because of the immense volume of debris, access to the front of the store was limited.

Cecil suddenly saw two very large black gentlemen standing at the front of the store in the pouring rain. They did not move around or change their stance or position. There was no motion with these men. They were just all of a sudden there. Cecil estimated the distance between where he stood just outside the storage room at the back of the store to where the men were standing at the front of the building to be about 50 feet. That distance, combined with the darkness from the pouring rain and the sky behind them, prevented Cecil from clearly distinguishing details of their faces or clothes. They were darkened silhouettes against a darker background.

Cecil could tell they stood facing into the store. The men were very tall, their height approaching the top of the now glass-free skeleton frame of the 7-foot-tall door jamb nearby. He noticed that the two men had very large, broad shoulders. Their stature reminded him of two bulky professional football players wearing shoulder pads. They looked like they would be very strong. He had no sense of fear from their presence, rather a quiet comfort, peace, and calm. The two men looked identical to each other, like carbon-copy twins. They stood quietly side by side, hands at their sides, just beyond where the front window of the store had stood minutes before. They did not call out. They did not utter a word. They did not move. They were just standing still.

Cecil felt peace and calm as he observed them standing there momentarily. It seemed to him they were assuring him, through their presence, that everything was going to be alright. He also felt they were guiding him away from the blocked access, away from the storefront, and instead to the hole in the south exterior wall of the building and the safety of the parking lot beyond.

After a few seconds, Cecil blinked, and the men were gone. The sense of calming peace remained. He was not aware of any sounds or noises from his surroundings, just quiet while they were present. That silence then stopped, and the normal sounds resumed as soon as the men were not visible. Cecil felt like the peace and strengthening comfort he experienced, and the detail of the directions he sensed in those few seconds, were actually much more in depth than could have been conveyed or comprehend in such abbreviated time. Later on, Cecil would look back on the experience and wonder why there seemed to be such a strong sense that he should exit the side of the building instead of the front.

Some of the people who had taken shelter in the restrooms were calling out for help. Once freed, they worked together to clear a path through the piles of debris scattered and strewn throughout the store. There were chairs, a sofa, televisions, large appliances, and the remnants of a collapsed interior wall in the large, open space of the store. There was a sizable opening in the wall on the south side of the building that would give them access to the parking lot.

When they had cleared enough of the debris to get safely out of the building, they stepped into the heavy rain. Cecil saw his car piled up with the rest of the vehicles on the parking lot; the lot resembled a salvage yard covered with damaged vehicles. He walked over to a triage area near 20th Street and Range Line Road and checked in briefly before heading across town to make sure his family was safe. The tornado and the peace he found within would prove to be an indelible event he would not soon forget.

◆ ◆ ◆

T he sun was shining brightly as Jim drove into town and up Range Line Road from the south. He had his car windows down and the sunroof open. There was a light breeze on that Sunday afternoon. The storm warning sirens had sounded briefly but then stopped. He noticed some dark clouds off to the west, but thought nothing of it. By the time he got out of his car at the 15th Street Wal-Mart, weather conditions were deteriorating. The sky to the west had grown pitch black. It looked like there was a large thunderstorm on its way through Joplin. The thought of an actual tornado did not cross his mind. As he walked in, the manager stopped Jim and told him there was a tornado spotted on the other side of town and told him he would need to go to the safe area at the back of the store. Jim looked past the manager through the door to see the sky had become dark with a greenish hue.

Jim agreed to go to the back of the store like everyone else and wait out the storm. He expected a 5-to-10-minute delay before he could finish his shopping. Nothing seemed extraordinarily unusual. He watched as the manager had to strongly convince a woman at the register that she needed to go to the back of the store like all the other people; she insisted she just needed to finish checking out so she could leave. Finally convinced, she relented and made her way to the back of the store. The manager's persistence may have saved the woman's life. There was certainly no safety or shelter outside. Even if she would have made it to her car, she would have never made it out of the parking lot. There was not enough time.

The front doors secured, customers in that area were hurried to the back of the store. People crowded together, standing elbow to elbow in the electronics department, layaway department, and public bathrooms near where Jim was standing. Other shoppers gathered near the middle of the store and in the rear of the grocery department. The employees worked to get everybody to the back of the building.

Almost immediately after Jim reached the electronics department, the lights inside the store flickered before going dark. He could hear the wind getting louder as the storm advanced toward the building. There was a swooshing sound and Jim watched as the store's suspended ceiling tiles would lift for a second then drop back into place. Then another swooshing sound and the ceiling tiles again lifted for a moment before they would move back into place. When the tiles dropped back into place the second time, there was a tremendous noise; Jim looked up to see the roof peel back as if a can opener had seamlessly removed it. As the roof lifted off, much of the structural support of the roof and walls disappeared, while the rest of the roof structure and walls collapsed into the store. Then the debris began to fly.

Just before the roof and walls collapsed, Jim noticed a woman and her young son a short distance from where he stood. There were several persons standing in between he and them. As the walls collapsed, Jim somehow ended up with the little boy in his arms and a shopping cart within his reach. He wasn't sure how the boy got into his arms, but he was able to cover the child and protect him from the debris. After the front wall of the storm had passed, many people thought that the storm was over and started moving around among the piles of scattered debris. Jim, though standing, was pinned between a DVD rack and a wall, the little boy still in his arms. He noticed the boy was not moving. He feared he had held him so tightly through the chaos that he had crushed him in his attempt to protect him. Within just a few more seconds, the pounding back wall of the storm came through. As another round of noise, debris, chaos, and destruction stormed, Jim's main concern was the well-being of the unmoving child in his arms. Within a few minutes, after the storm had finally passed, he felt a nudge as the boy began to stir and then finally awaken. The boy had been in shock. He was not injured, to Jim's great relief. The child's mother made it over to Jim to find her son safe.

The people began to dig themselves and others out from under piles of debris. They were all covered with messy debris and soaked to the bone from the cold rain that followed the storm. Jim saw the concrete block wall that had been standing just behind him had fallen into the store. The storeroom behind the main part of the store was visible and he could see stacks of industrial shelves partially supporting sections of fallen wall.

People worked together to dig out a woman who suffered a broken back. A store employee grabbed a shelf, and a few men moved the woman onto it. People provided their belts to secure the woman to the shelf to immobilize her. With a calm sense of clarity, everyone worked together to help get through the situation they were in.

The men found another gentleman pinned behind a wall, under a steel roof joist and some sheet rock. The men were able to lift the steel beam a few inches to allow him to crawl out. The people in what had previously been the electronics department were hemmed in by massive piles of debris on all sides. There was not much choice of which direction they could go to get safely out. The shortest, most direct route to safety was to the east. After they had freed as many people as they could see in close proximity, people started to build a ramp from the debris, up to the collapsed wall just behind them. If they could get over the wall, they could be safely out of the store.

As the people were working to build the ramp, Jim noticed that two black gentlemen showed up on top of the industrial shelves and walked down to where the people in the electronics department were gathered. There was something about their appearance that seemed unusual, or at least unexpected. Both gentlemen were tall. They both had on khaki, cargo-type shorts with frayed hems, neither had on a shirt or shoes, and both were in amazing physical shape. "If you worked out daily for many months, you still would not have the perfect bodies of these two men," Jim said. "They were built like tanks, like skin over steel. They had a chiseled appearance. They looked like angelic statues. They were both very clean, absent of any of the pieces of insulation, mud, or debris covering all the other people in the wreckage of the store. They looked alike. They dressed alike. They acted alike. They just showed up at the top of the shelves."

When the debris pile ramp grew tall enough, people were able to climb up onto the wall to get out. Several gentlemen lined up on top of the wall to help. The two large, black gentlemen were spaced apart on the human line formed on the debris ramp. Several of the men would help people up onto the debris ramp where the two large gentlemen would help them up from one to the other, and finally to the men on top of the wall to help the people over to safety, much like a bucket brigade. When it came to the woman with the broken back, 3 or 4 of the men would lift the shelf holding the woman and hand her up to the first large gentleman. He would, by himself, take the woman and hand it to the second large gentleman above him on the wall. That second gentleman would then take the shelf with the woman in his arms by himself, and lift it up to the 2 or 3 men on top of the wall. Those gentlemen on top would then take the woman on over the wall to safety.

The two large gentlemen were incredibly strong and seemed to have no sense of the weight they were lifting. They did not appear to strain, even with the heavier people they were helping. They seemed to have limitless strength. Where it took several men to lift the woman with the back injury, these two gentlemen could handle the task by themselves, with no help from anyone else. The lifting went on non-stop for more than an hour. They showed no sign of wearing down or fatigue. During that time, Jim did not hear the two gentlemen speak, not even to each other. He noticed no communication between them for the entire hour. They were just there.

Periodically, Jim, with another gentleman, would climb onto the industrial shelves standing behind the wall to use it as an observation point to see if there were other areas inside the store where they might be able to help. When they had finally finished getting everybody they could see and reach out, Jim wanted to thank the two large gentlemen for all their help moving 40 to 50 people to safety. The two gentlemen had just climbed back onto the shelves near where Jim first noticed them. He climbed up as well, but when he reached the top shelf, they were not there. He was standing by himself. He could see some other people still working, but he saw no sign of these two gentlemen. He saw no sign of them beyond the wall. He saw no sign of them inside the twisted wreckage of the mangled store. Because of their appearance, they should have been easy to find.

"You just don't lose two gentlemen such as these! They just went over that wall and disappeared. It was as if the wall marked the beginning and the end of their presence."

Jim wondered aloud about these two gentlemen he believed to be angels. Why were they there? Why were they there instead of somewhere else? Why now? Why were they helping these people? The reason they were there at that point in time was not easily pinpointed. Jim said that, from his perception, he believes, "Man wants to be able to touch something or feel it, to be able to comprehend it or understand it. We want to be able to grasp it or have something tangible that explains why it happened. Could the reason for these two large gentlemen to be here and now be due to the massive amount of damage? If they are here, are they other places too? Was it due to the death and destruction? There was plenty of that all around, not just here or now. Was it because they came as an answer to prayers?"

Jim saw people act in a way that day that he wished they would every day. Though the storm seemed to bring out the worst in some people, he saw that it also brought out the very best in many others.

Jim said, "Under normal circumstances, people, myself included, might have little to nothing to do with somebody in need. We would be like the priest in the 'Good Samaritan' parable, crossing to the other side of the road, rather than be placed in front of the person in need. On the day of the storm, I saw people look for a piece of cloth in the rubble, dig it out and shake out the loose debris, and reach over and wipe the face of a complete stranger and offer them comfort and consolation, doing whatever they could to help the true Spirit shine through." He saw that characteristic in the way he found himself helping those around him as well.

Though the storm brought a lion's share of death and destruction to Joplin, Jim saw a shining vein of peace, love, and compassion. "There was more than chaos and confusion," Jim said. "I was able to see joy. I saw promise. There were so many positive things that I saw take place that day that just happened to be wrapped up in some pretty large negative things." He recognized there was much more to the dynamics when you look beneath those things on the surface.

Jim says that he was blessed with what he saw take place that day inside the Wal-Mart store. He saw human spirit, stretched far above and beyond what he ever imagined possible.

❖ ❖ ❖

Zach stopped at Wal-Mart on 15th Street with his children, William, 11, and Kate, 8, to buy some groceries before going to church. He began his shopping back in the dairy section and gradually worked his way to the front of the store. He was just getting to the bakery counter when he noticed some commotion among the store managers. He watched them as they gathered for a few moments near the front entrance then spread out to talk to the customers nearby. Zach noticed the sky outside through the front glass doors was considerably darker than when he came in about 30 minutes earlier. It looked like a storm was approaching. Two store employees locked the front doors. There were a number of people who had just gone through the checkout line or were still standing in line to do so. Some argued with the employees that they wanted out of the store and would not stay. Others complained it was such an inconvenience for them to have to wait around. Though some insisted on leaving the store, most of the customers stayed. As Zach watched, he was deciding if he, too, was going to stay or leave. A store employee then approached him and warned him and his children of the impending storm. He decided to stay.

Employees formed a line and systematically moved through each aisle of the store to alert every customer. The staff members were directing everybody to the safe room in the back. Zach pushed his shopping cart without haste, not in step with the brisk pace of the employees. Zach saw no people missed or left behind. Everyone seemed to hurry to the back of the store. Fawn, the children's mother, was trying to get in touch with Zach by cell phone to warn him of the impending storm, but the cell towers, by then, had already become a casualty of the storm and the service was down. She was finally able to reach him through her mother in California. Zach looked at the weather radar on the small screen of his cell phone and noticed the storm cell had a clear hook feature. At the time, he did not think too much about the severity of the storm or whether it would possibly have any effect on him.

As Zach turned into the main aisle that stretched across the back half of the store, he saw that the designated safe areas of the electronics and layaway departments were already full. People were starting to spill out into the aisles adjacent to and leading up to the layaway department, with some still standing in the main aisle. The aisles on both sides of the layaway department—one in the toy department, the other in the electronics department—were nearly full. Many people were down on their hands and knees. Zach estimated there were about 200 people in that area.

As the aisles began to overflow with people, Zach discarded his full grocery cart and guided his children to the electronics department to look for protective shelter there. They were within a 20-foot radius from the checkout counter in the center of the department. Zach led his children to a spot near the central checkout counter and got down on the floor between two aisles; the department crowded with people. He had William and Kate lie down on their backs facing him and laid over them. Zach hugged both as closely as he could. Moments before the storm hit, there was an influx of people into the electronics department. The people were from a nearby trailer park and had been instructed to head for Wal-Mart in case of a tornado, though, in the end, it never hit their trailer park. From his vantage point, Zach could see all the people coming in, as they ran past him towards the layaway department.

The storm hit the front of the store about 5 minutes after the managers first began to move the customers to the back of the building. As Zach heard the storm begin to hit, he eyed the checkout counter a few feet away. He thought that it may have been bolted to the floor and more secure than where he was. He scooted his children across the floor and against the back side of the counter. He again laid over them and hugged them as tightly as he could, up against the side of the counter. Zach told them to get underneath him as much as they were able as he tried to cover them up completely. He looked around to see if there was anything nearby that he could hold onto but there was nothing to be found. He heard a lot of people around him making peace with God that day. He could hear their prayers and cries as the storm closed in.

Zach prayed to God, "This is on you, save my kids." There

was nothing he could have done to change his circumstances. Whatever happened from that point was completely out of his control, but he was at peace.

Zach looked to his right and saw a woman next to him with her teenage daughter. The woman had dumped her shopping cart upside down and put it over her daughter, then laid down on the floor next to her as the storm hit. All the lights inside the store went dark. The noise was deafening as the building ripped open. It sounded like a machine eating the building. Above the noise of the storm, people began to scream.

The roof peeled back exposing the open sky. All the roof covering was gone and the superstructure was either collapsed or missing. There were loud creaking, grinding, unsettling noises as the roof panels were peeled and the beams stressed and bent. There were thunderous crashes all around.

The wind stopped almost immediately as the eye passed overhead. Zach hoped it was over and lifted his head to look around. He then looked up and was able to see into the eye inside the funnel. He could clearly see the blue sky above the cloud, surrounded by the dark gray walls of the inside of the storm. The debris inside the wall of the storm was rotating counterclockwise above him. He saw what he thought to be a large piece of plastic circling inside the middle of the eye. It seemed to be just floating somewhat aimlessly in a clockwise direction. Zach was still being pelted in the face with small bits of debris. He felt it sting like a pellet or a BB might. The small pelting debris stopped momentarily to be replaced by a light calm breeze blowing on his face. It was almost refreshing and peaceful in the midst of all the damage surrounding him.

The tiny debris flying through the air filled his children's ears and noses—Fawn would later have to scrub repeatedly to work it all out. Zach had tiny pieces of debris embedded into the leather of his back pocket wallet—the debris could not be removed, even with tweezers.

The calmness of the eye did not last long. Zach could see the back wall of the inside of the storm approach, and he began to hear it devour what was left of the building. The noise level shot up dramatically. Zach put his head back down close to the children and yelled to them that he loved them. He was comforted to hear them respond. He knew there was a significant chance he was not going to survive the storm. The back half of the storm was much worse in comparison to the front half. The sound level was twice as loud. He could hear the bulky air conditioners crashing into the store. He could feel the thud of something large as it crashed very close to where he was huddled over his children. He thought at first it might have hit him because it was so close, but it was the concussion from the tremendous impact.

Through the deafening winds, Zach could hear people praying loudly. More ear-piercing crashes resounded and some of the praying voices would stop. Sometimes, the voices would start back up. Sometimes, they would not. It seemed to go on for an extraordinary length of time.

As soon as the storm winds passed, Zach heard William lying beneath him gargling and saying, "I can't breathe! I can't breathe!" Zach shifted his weight to make sure he was not crushing his son. As he reached down to move, he could see they were laying in several inches of water. He lifted William's head above the water so he could breathe freely. As Zach shifted to give William some more room, his back bumped against a light pole that had pulled from the parking lot and come to rest over the checkout counter. There was an incredibly long steel girder laid over top of the light pole. These steel poles formed an "X" directly over their heads. There was no part of the roof remaining directly above them.

As people began to crawl out from under the debris,

somebody started to yell out, "Hail! Hail! Hail!" Everybody retreated into their debris covered holes to wait out the hailstorm. There was nowhere for Zach to go to get his children out of the pounding hail. He lay back down over them to protect them with his body for a little while longer. He tried to cover his own head as best he could, but he was pounded relentlessly by the hail for 4 more minutes. When the hail finally stopped, Zach looked over toward the teenage daughter whose mother had placed her under a shopping cart. He noticed the shopping cart had a huge dent on the corner just above the daughter's head. The mother and daughter were both alright. The shopping cart may have saved her life. Zach tried to move to his left and was blocked by debris. He tried to move to his right but was hindered again.

Zach saw a hole, about the size of a milk crate, through the rubble in front of him. As soon as the hail stopped, while still stuck under the debris, a black and white dog wedged its head in through the hole and began licking William's face for a moment or two. As soon as the dog finished licking William's face, it turned its attention to Kate and did the same thing. After that, it licked Zach on the face. When the dog finished licking him, Zach watched as it worked its way around to the girl underneath the shopping cart. The dog walked up to the overturned shopping cart and stuck its head inside and licked the girl on the face for a moment, then on to the girl's mother. From his vantage point, under the debris, Zach could see the dog go from one person, to another, to another, to another, and do the same thing with each one of them. The dog would lick the person on the face until they became more alert and responsive, then it would move on to the next person and do the same. It was a medium to large-sized, long-haired dog, resembling a collie mix or large labrador-german shepherd mix. It did not have any identification or marking indicating it was a service or rescue dog.

Zach shoved some of the rubble out of the way to clear the

hole, then pushed his children through as he followed behind. There were mountains of debris surrounding him as he stood. Zach estimates the size of the pocket around them was only about 30 to 40 feet across. There was a wall of debris between him and the southern wall of the area where the DVDs and video games had been located. Because of the huge debris piles, he was unable to see to the layaway department located between the toys and electronics, where people had taken shelter. He had no idea of their fate. He did not know that the people in that area ended up going over the back wall of the store to safety.

Zach's attention shifted back to the canine and he noticed a young girl by the dog, wearing a knee-length red raincoat with blue jeans underneath. The raincoat, with the hood pulled up over her head, was clean and dry. She just stood in one place on a small pile of debris, while the dog systematically went from person to person in the immediate area. Zach did not recall the girl moving from where she stood. She had a red leash in her hand, but it was not attached to the dog.

As the dog went from person to person, the girl stood in one place and repeated, "She won't bite. She won't bite. She won't bite." The appearance of the girl stood out because she was not wet or debris-covered like everyone else. The girl's tone never changed as she repeated her comforting words. There was no fear, anxiety, or concern in the girl's voice. Zach felt as if the girl was there to provide comfort to the people. Of the 18 to 20 people in the area, Zach watched as the dog licked the faces of about 10 to 12 of them.

Zach later wondered how the dog came to be in the battered store. He recalled the minutes immediately before the storm while he was with his children near the bakery counter. He observed the front door for several minutes and could see every person who entered during that time. Moving to the back of the store, he observed that no one was left behind and that there was no girl with a dog.

There was no girl with a dog in the electronics department when Zach and his children reached the area. When the store employee went back to the front door to allow the people from the trailer park to come inside, Zach could see everyone who ran down the center aisle, and there was no dog. The lights were still on right up until the storm hit the front of the building. He had no idea how the dog could have gotten there. He considered it may have come into the store during the storm but quickly discounted that as well. Zach noticed this dog was not injured or in shock. It just went calmly and methodically from one person to another. If it came in from the storm, it would have been injured by the massive amount of flying debris. Then there was the girl in the raincoat. Why would she be wearing a raincoat? The weather outside just 5 minutes beforehand was very hot and dry. The cleanliness of her clothes stood out among all the people Zach could see. Everyone was covered with a debris slurry from the top of their heads down to their feet. Everyone was soaked to the bone from the 4 to 6 inches of rain that came with the storm. She was clean and dry.

Like Zach and his children, Randy and his wife, Stacy, were also in the store shopping when the storm hit. They both ended up seeking shelter in the store's designated safe areas. They finally ended up in the electronics department in the same general vicinity as Zach by the time the storm hit the store. They were there with their sons, Levi, 10, Austin, 9, and Christian, 8. Stacy had ended up with severe injuries and was not able to get out of the debris-filled store under her own power. When asked if they remembered seeing a dog in the electronics department, to their parents' surprise, both Levi and Austin said they remembered seeing a dog in the area immediately after the storm. Neither Randy, Stacy, nor Christian could recall seeing the dog. When asked to describe the dog as best they could, both of the boys described seeing a large black and white dog walking around. Both of the boys remembered petting the dog as it walked by them at some point. Neither of the two boys remembered seeing the girl or anyone else with the dog.

There was actually a dog let into the store just moments before the storm. A woman, in her 50s or 60s, came from the parking lot near the grocery store entrance just before the storm hit, seeking shelter with her dog. The dog, a large, yellow labrador retriever–like breed ended up in the area just north of where Zach and his children sought protection. The dog had been separated from the woman briefly during the chaos of the storm, but was re-united shortly after the storm passed. The descriptions of the color of the dog by Zach, William, Kate, Levi, and Austin were all the same, and nothing like the woman's yellow dog. The demeanor of the dog they all described was also nothing like a dog who pulled loose, scared of the storm. The dog Zach and the children watched in the electronics department seemed totally unfazed by the storm.

People were still trying to come to terms with what they had just experienced, standing there in the middle of the vast pile of debris. The sky was beginning to lighten up again as the main part of the storm continued eastward. Some people were starting to become frantic, looking for family members still buried under debris. Others were trying to climb over the immediate debris piles to see what they may be able to do to get out of the wreckage, but there was no easy way out. All in all, it was becoming much more chaotic as people were trying to figure out what to do next. There were alarms and bells and whistles going off throughout the store adding to the confusion. Zach remembers one of the sirens gave out an eerie sound, as if it was under water. He was still near the back wall of the store but could not exactly see where the sound came from. Though, it could have come from the nearby apartment complex where he noticed people climbing out of the wreckage from the top floors. Zach remembers seeing one little girl moving around with her arms raised in the air, praising Jesus repeatedly. There were about 18 to 20 people in all who stood up in the electronics department after the storm.

Zach looked around to see where the girl in the raincoat and the dog were. There was no visible way for them to get out of the immediate area, yet they were nowhere to be found. They were gone.

It was now time to find a way out of the store. People helped each other navigate through hanging wires, twisted shelves, and strewn merchandise. They climbed over, under, or through barriers of fallen debris as they made their way to the front of the store. The journey took between 45 minutes and an hour.

When Zach and his children reached the parking lot, his car, once parked in front of the lawn and garden department, was now relocated to the north end of the parking lot over 500 feet away. It was found on top of 3 cars and underneath 4 more. He pulled himself up to look into it to make sure it was really his car. It was. Thankfully, he and his children were able to get a ride to his home 6 blocks away.

CHAPTER 19
BUTTERFLIES

"Then I raised my eyes and looked, and there were two women, coming with the wind in their wings; for they had wings like the wings of a stork, and they lifted up the basket between earth and heaven."—**Zechariah 5:9 (NKJV)**

Most of the appearances of an angel in the Bible are in the form of a man. Zechariah 5:9 is the only verse found describing an angel as a woman with wings.

The numerous butterfly stories, or butterfly people stories, coming to surface after the storm are intriguing. The stories spread quickly among the people of Joplin and Duquesne, Missouri. Like many of the countless stories that were told and retold across the city in the days, weeks, and months after the storm, the butterfly stories were uplifting and offered plenty of hope and encouragement.

There were many stories that were heard. In one instance, a mother and her young daughter were in their car when they saw the approaching tornado. They had just enough time to get out of the car and into a ditch, where the mother laid over the daughter. After the storm had passed, the mother checked on her daughter's condition asking is she was alright. The daughter exclaimed, "Oh, yes, weren't they beautiful?" When the mother asked what the daughter was talking about, she answered, "Didn't you see how beautiful the wings on the butterfly women were? They were all around us." The daughter went on to tell her mother that the butterfly people were around some of the other people taking shelter nearby as well. The child was not described as fearful at what she saw.

In another story, the father of a small child had just enough time to get his child into the bathtub before the storm smashed into his house. The child was on their back in the bathtub as the father laid over them, face down. When the storm struck, the bathroom ceiling was peeled away and the walls strained in the wind. As the storm was overhead, the father was lifted into the air above the tub, hanging on as best as he could. After a few seconds, he would be drawn back down over his child. In another moment, he would be lifted up into the air, and then pulled back down. After the storm, the child—having been able to see the sky above and behind the father—would tell him that the butterfly people were on the father's back, pushing him back down into the tub, to keep him from floating away. The child would describe the beautiful wings like a butterfly. This child, as with the other butterfly people stories from children, was not scared of what they saw and described.

In the many interviews I, Dr. Brothers, and my wife, Rosie conducted, the butterfly stories proved the most difficult to track down. We became aware of several reasons why the firsthand stories were so elusive. Nearly all the butterfly stories we heard involved the testimony of very young children. Rather than spending too much time trying to assess why the butterfly stories were all from children's accounts, we would rather just acknowledge that aspect and move on. Many storm stories in this book started out as second-person accounts from adults, but the children's butterfly stories were always third-person stories. The adult stories often included a name or an employer as reference, somebody we could actually track down. The children's butterfly stories were always about an obscure child, with no name or other reference. Just because there were not names associated with the butterfly stories did not invalidate the stories or diminish the truth. In actuality, we were able to find some of the stories, but they have remained mostly inaccessible.

One standard we held for every one of our interviews was that the story had to be "first person" to be included in this book. We only wanted to talk to the person who actually saw, heard, or experienced the event, and not the person who heard about it from another person. With the butterfly stories, we were willing to make an exception of the first-person requirement by including the testimony from the child's parent as the source instead. We even considered including "non-counselor" conversations that some of the area pastors may have heard from the children firsthand, but ultimately decided against that option.

This storm was not a pretty storm. There were many things about the events that day that were very ugly. There were horrific things that took place. Even many seasoned health care workers accustomed to dealing routinely with traumatic injuries and tragedy through their jobs were very strongly impacted by the things they witnessed that day. Many of the people who are normally isolated or insulated from such events found themselves right in the middle of the traumatic disaster, in a very up close and personal manner. They would see, hear, smell, and feel things that will be seared into their memory for many years to come. This also included the children. There was a lot of pain associated with this storm. Many individuals and families sought guidance and comfort through numerous private, school, or pastoral counselors. We talked to more than a dozen counselors and pastors who worked with some of the children firsthand after the storm. The counselors assured us they had heard the butterfly stories firsthand from the children. They do exist. I have no reason to doubt the existence or the content of the dozens and dozens of the butterfly people stories.

There were skeptical reporters whose articles would try to discredit the possibility of truth in the children's stories. There were reports from counselors who would insist their professional training would lead them to conclude the child was fabricating the experience to help cope with the trauma. I don't know how many of the stories actually exist. Are there 20? Maybe 30? Maybe 50? No one knows for sure. Can an "expert" easily discredit all of the butterfly stories with a single swipe? How could so many children come up with the same concept independently at the same time? Why would all the children lie? Why would they all make up similar stories? Do they have a class for this at the daycare level? Could the person in the Bible verse at the beginning of this chapter possibly be mistaken for a butterfly? Or is only "stork" acceptable? If an expert disagrees with the testimony, does it necessarily qualify it as a lie?

If a person can only believe in the existence of what he sees, how can he believe in the existence of the wind or even the air he breathes? You can't see gravity. Does it exist? How about angels? How about God? It would seem easier to just accept that the children saw what they said they saw. I believe the children for the most part saw what they said they saw and did their best to describe their experience in terms they understand.

We do not want to prolong that healing process for those families, and I would encourage everybody to include those families in your prayers.

CHAPTER 20
GOD'S PEACE

"And He stayed in the wilderness (desert) forty days, being tempted [all the while] by Satan; and He was with the wild beasts, and the angels ministered to Him [continually]."—**Mark 1:13 (AMPC)**

J errye had gone to church like she did every Sunday. Her friend, Arlie, would usually go to his stepdaughter's house on Sunday evening for dinner; on this Sunday, Arlie called Jerrye to let her know that his stepdaughter was not going to be cooking that evening. Jerrye then invited Arlie over for some barbeque sandwiches and coleslaw for dinner.

Arlie arrived at Jerrye's house just west of St. John's Hospital shortly after and parked his car in the driveway. The television was on in the living room when Arlie arrived, tuned to a local channel, but the volume was turned way down. Neither Jerrye nor Arlie had any idea a huge storm was rapidly forming just a mile or so west of them and was a few minutes away. They could not hear the storm warning sirens from inside the house.

Jerrye's house was only about 8 blocks from Schifferdecker Avenue, and 4 blocks from the storm siren located near Cecil Floyd Elementary School. The electricity would have gone out very soon after the siren sounded, the warning being audible for only a few seconds before the power would be lost.

As they sat in the dining room, Jerrye could see out the west-facing window that clouds were rapidly getting darker to the west and the wind was starting to pick up. She was concerned a limb from the large pecan tree or the maple tree in the front yard might blow back and hit the dining room window—she reasoned there would be glass all over the table, so she closed the blinds. She had no idea a tornado was grinding through the neighborhood and was only a few blocks away.

As she reached the window, Jerrye could hear the deep roaring sound of a freight train associated with tornadoes. Even though she had never been in a tornado, Jerrye knew exactly what was causing the sound. In all the commotion Jerrye was not aware when the electricity went out. It was time to get to safety. Arlie had not even finished his sandwich when he and Jerrye went down the hall toward the back of the house. Arriving at the bathroom they moved inside and closed the door. Sitting there, they could hear things smashing into the side of the house. The noise quickly increased in volume. Within just a few seconds, the freight train sound had grown to sound more like a 747-jumbo jet as the force of the wind pounded the side of the house with debris. Jerrye could hear glass breaking, tree limbs snapping, and the splintering of wooden boards. The noise was incredible.

As they sat on the floor in the darkness of the bathroom, Jerrye put her head down on her arms and prayed to God, "Whatever You want, I am ready." She immediately felt a calm, peaceful warmth come over her. Even though the noise raged outside, Jerrye felt no anxiety or fear. She believes, "The feeling of peace, warmth, and calm in the bathroom was from an angel or from the presence of God. That incredible sense of peace, calm, and warmth lasted until well after the storm had passed."

There were changes in the noise level, but the sound never completely stopped as in the storm's eye. Jerrye's house was just on the north edge of the storm, so the eye missed the house just to the south. After the initial blast of destructive winds passed, the noise level inside the house fluctuated somewhere between very loud and extremely loud. As the storm passed, Jerrye did not feel like the back portion of the storm lasted as long as the front portion.

It had sounded like the whole roof was coming off the house during the storm. When Jerrye opened the bathroom door, she saw the floor in the hallway and into the living room was covered with leaves and other small debris. She told Arlie the yard was now in the front living room. The bottom panel of her garage door had been blown in by the strong winds. With the garage door panel gone, the force of the wind blowing into the garage blew the door into the kitchen wide open. The garage then acted like a funnel, allowing the wind to blow debris into the house.

There had been a limb or board that broke through the outside east wall of the back bedroom, before being pulled out, leaving a hole in the wall. She had lost only one window in the front of the house. There was another 4-foot hole in the garage above her car where she could see daylight through the broken rafter joists and missing sheet rock. Her home had been spared the direct hit of the destructive winds, but her neighbor's houses, just two or three doors down and only 150 feet away, suffered extensive damage or were totally destroyed. With their location just on the north side of the storm, most of the direct force of the wind was initially from the southeast and then shifted from the northeast as the storm passed by. The pecan tree in the front yard had fallen to the southwest into the empty street. As large as the tree was, had it fallen on anything—car or building—it would have most likely completely crushed or flattened whatever was underneath it.

Arlie told Jerrye the barbeque sandwich ended up costing him $17,000. His car, parked in the driveway, was totaled by the wind-driven hail and debris.

When Jerrye hears people ask, "Where was God," Jerrye answers them with, "You better believe that He was here. According to the Bible, God knows exactly when each of our times are up. We are either finished with our work here or we are not. Either way, our time is our time." She feels tremendously blessed she was spared any further damage.

◆ ◆ ◆

I n his mind, Tom has gone over and over the tangled events of that Sunday in May. As he looks back on all that transpired throughout that day, he begins to see how precisely—even very minute things—fit together to become an intricate part of a much bigger picture.

Tom and his daughter, Olivia, 11, had just left church at College Heights Christian School in Joplin, Missouri that morning. Normally, Olivia would go back to her mother's house after church. Today, the plans were different. Tom and Olivia would go to lunch together to celebrate Olivia's final straight-A report card for a perfect year, and would spend the rest of the afternoon and evening at his home.

About 3 p.m., Tom and Olivia went to Cunningham Park, just blocks east of Tom's home, to play some tennis. After about 45 minutes or so, the heat and humidity were almost unbearable, so they decided to head home. Tom noticed there was something very different about the air. It felt heavy and thick, almost like soup.

After they got home, Tom and Olivia sat around relaxing and having a snack when the storm warning sirens—located just a few blocks up the hill—sounded for a moment or two then stopped. They did what many people that day did when they heard the storm siren sound, they went outside to look at the sky. They could see the darker sky through the tall trees near Tom's home, but it looked like it was quite a distance away at the time. Tom took a couple of pictures. He reasoned that, if there was an actual tornado, his home, located down in a valley, would be fairly protected. He was not overly concerned, so they both went back inside.

Tom turned the television on to check the weather report, interested to see if there was a serious storm and exactly where it was headed. There was no unusual reason for safety concerns, much less fear; there had been many storm warning sirens sounded in Joplin before. When Tom looked at the radar image on television, he saw the rapidly increasing intensity of the storm just west of town. He had no idea of the proximity of the massive storm until the lights flickered off and on a moment later. Then he heard the second siren.

Tom quickly reasoned it was foolish to not do anything about the safety, security, and well being of both he and Olivia. Tom realized he was showing his daughter absolutely no sense of personal responsibility in potentially dangerous situations. He also recognized that he had never shown her where to seek shelter or what to look for in a safety zone.

They hurried to the bathroom under the stairwell. The small room, measuring about 4 by about 6 to 7-foot, was probably initially designed as a storage cubby under the stairs, just off the kitchen, but was later converted to a compact half bath. The ceiling sloped down steeply from the stairway above. It was a very tight space for a single adult, even more so when paired with a child. Olivia sat on the toilet while Tom stood with his back to the closed door. Then the lights went off for the last time. He believed they would be alright in the bathroom. He remembers that, when the lights went off, it was pitch black. There was no light coming through the blinds on the window across the room at all.

Within a matter of 10 to 15 seconds, the second siren stopped from loss of power. They huddled in the tiny bathroom. The lights were out. They could both hear a sound like a freight train. It turned out that they had little time to spare. Tom recognized there was some very intense wind, but still reasoned his home in a valley would be spared. Then it all broke loose.

Olivia was hunched down as low as she could get on the toilet. Tom was hovering over her as best he could, and he began to pray. The noise was deafening. He could not hear Olivia. He did not know if she was crying or what her condition was. He was not even sure if she was still there at that point. He could feel the swirling wind around him become disoriented in the chaos, losing all sense of where he was. The deafening roar masked any sounds of specific destruction taking place around them. He prayed over and over, if God was to take them, "Do it quickly with no suffering." He felt his time was over and there was no way out. He felt the stairwell against his back as it collapsed down on top of them. The bathroom door he had held onto so tightly twisted and torqued in the frame, pulling free from his grip, torn out by the hinges, and disappearing immediately into the blackness of the storm. He believed he would probably follow the same path in the next few seconds. The compression of the stairwell, and whatever else was left above, essentially kept them secured in the last standing structure of their home.

His home was located close to the northern wall of the eye of the storm. They felt the quiet of the eye of the storm for about 30 seconds before the wind and the vacuum started back up. Some of the debris that piled on top of them began to pull loose and be picked up by the winds of the back wall of the storm. He could feel that both he and Olivia were being lifted from the ground with the debris above them.

By the time the destruction was over, they had been buried under 6 to 7 feet of debris. They could see a light shine down on them through the pile. They did not know where they were but believed they would need to somehow crawl out and go toward the light above them. Olivia would climb up and out first. Tom was all twisted and turned around under the debris that was just

5 minutes before his stairwell and bathroom. When Olivia was able to climb up to the top of the pile and stick her head out into the heavy rain, Tom could see from the look on her face that things outside were very different. She started crying at what she saw, asking if it was a dream. Tom began to climb out. He had gym shorts on with no shoes. His shirt was torn to ribbons. As he was climbing out, his phone dropped out of his pocket and he climbed back to retrieve it. As soon as he got up out of the hole it began to hail.

They could now hear the neighbors next door crying out for help. The neighbors had also sought shelter under their stairwell, but both were blown out onto the kitchen floor as the stairwell vanished into the wind—they were protected by a piece of plywood that had blown on top of them. By the time they were getting their senses about them, the heavy rain began to pick up and the hail intensified. There was a lot of lightning in the air for the next 5 to 6 minutes. They ran to their cars still parked just east of the home for shelter from the lightning and hail. When they got out of the cars, they saw many people waving boards from under the debris calling for help. Tom found one sandal and one dress shoe in the rubble he could wear to protect his feet from the nails and glass that covered the ground all around him.

Tom said he had been faced with knowing this could be the end. Unlike a car accident that has immediate results, he had time to think. His biggest concern, part of what he calls the human equation, was that he did not want to be in pain. He did not want to suffer. He did not want to go separately from his daughter. He knows how the big story ends and he is alright with it. He processed many thought in that short time. He believes there are many people, even some very strong Christians, harboring doubts in their minds when confronted with situations like these. Those same doubts raced through his mind.

Tom had been praying the next night to be able to find a

bowl holding his money clip and all of his identification, credit cards, Social Security card, and driver's license. It may have seemed selfish, but it would help simplify some of the challenges that lay immediately ahead of him. He had been looking through the debris before and found there was almost nothing useable in the rubble. About 15 minutes after he arrived that next morning, he was able to look down in the debris to where he last saw the bowl. He could see that, laying in a straight row behind the bowl, were the credit cards, driver's license, identification, Social Security card, and the empty money clip. Talking to his parents a week later, Tom recalled how his mother told him she had a favorite picture he had found at a yard sale that meant a lot to her. His dad told Tom of a watch he had bought and wishes that it would have been found as well. Tom went back the next day after AmeriCorps had cleaned the lot and, there on the cleaned foundation, was both the picture and the watch. Those few small rewards helped him continue to pray about being faithful and thankful for God's continual presence through it all. He considers himself to be very blessed.

Tom recognizes the debris had to fall perfectly into place for them to be shielded from injury in the destruction. The large appliances from the kitchen had to fall in precisely the right spot to support the debris that landed on top of it in such a way to give them a beacon of light to climb toward for safety. Like many of the homes in the rest of Joplin, all that remained of Tom's home was the spot where they were located. Nothing else of any substance was left standing. He said that, if Olivia had not been at his home that day, he would have reacted to the storm differently. He said he would have probably been lying on the couch in the front room. The couch ended up with a 20-foot-long steel I-beam sticking through it. Olivia's presence altered his decisions that day and most likely saved his life. He recognized the incredible short time he had available to make life-saving decisions, only about 15 seconds or so.

When he looks at how all the pieces fell, literally, he feels the peace that was brought upon him that day; even amid the chaos, there was as much peace from God as could be absorbed.

Tom believes God had something very specific in mind for each person who went through the storm that day. There will always be questions and debates about the storm. Why would God do this? Why did He not intervene here and prevent this from happening? Why this person? Why not that person? There could be no answers. Tom trusts he would have been taken care of no matter what. God would protect and sustain here or bring us home and reward us with, "Job well done, faithful servants."

The churches would now have the opportunity to put down their individual banners and care for people in need, doing what churches are commissioned to do. Those looking in from the outside could now have the opportunity to see what churches are made of. They could see the hands and feet and heart of God at work.

Tom has a renewed intensity to roll up his sleeves and get out on the streets and serve others. Tom and Olivia feel they have been given a new opportunity to hone the path laid out in front of them because of the storm. Olivia was baptized a month later. They have a fervency and joy in their service to others. The normal was not bad before, but the new normal is much different. Tom doesn't miss what was lost, because the experience was what he needed to actually get out and effectively reach others.

◆ ◆ ◆

Pat was taking it easy in the living room of her two-story home near St. Mary's Church that Sunday afternoon, dressed comfortably in capri pants, sandals, and a T-shirt. She was watching the Hallmark Channel on television. Since local weather reports are not broadcast on this channel as they are with local channel programming, Pat had no idea of the severe weather forming just a few miles away.

Pat became aware that the winds were picking up noticeably that afternoon, but did not notice the storm warning sirens. The sky had darkened considerably but was not giving much cause for alarm. However, Pat did take notice when she looked outside her living room window and saw the rain begin to really intensify, with golf ball-sized hail mixed in. The possibility of worse weather did not cause Pat much alarm, an actual tornado was not even a consideration. She walked into the dining room located on the southwest corner of her house and closed the window. She then walked over to the west-facing sliding glass patio door to close it as well. As she was closing the door, Pat heard a window break in the upstairs bedroom, but was still not overly concerned. She knew there was a tall tree growing near the house on the west side of the building and assumed a tree branch had blown against the window, breaking it. She would just head upstairs to secure the broken glass window and cover it with a box or something. It was not really a big deal at the time. She had no idea the front face of a destructive, monstrous storm was only about a block away.

As Pat walked toward the staircase to go upstairs and tend to the broken window, she looked over her shoulder and out the glass door she had just closed in time to see her wicker settee on the patio take off like a jet, northward into the sky. Pat was taken by what she saw. She began to process everything in her mind and was acutely aware that she needed to get to a safe area quickly. She made a beeline into a closet that was directly ahead of her, about 5 to 6 feet away, under the stairway. She had no time to waste as the storm crashed in on the house. She literally had less than 2 seconds to make it into the closet and pull the door shut. There was no time to think what her options were. There was no time to spare. She had no more than pulled the door closed when the house outside the closet exploded. The closet was very small, and the ceiling sloped down from the stairway above. The hot water tank took up about one-half to one-third of the taller front part of the closet. The vacuum cleaner took up a little of the floor space as well. The rest of the space was further reduced by a couple of folding chairs that had been stored there, as well as the extra leaf for the dining room table. Pat had just enough room in that tiny closet to be able to stand in one spot. She said that, "For some unknown reason, the closet would have normally been cluttered, but on this particular afternoon, was clean."

The tremendous noise started up immediately once she got into the closet. The loud noises coming from outside the space sounded like a huge monster, roaring as it devoured the house piece by piece. There was the sound of wooden boards being splintered and glass cracking and shattering. As Pat hung on to the trembling door handle under the darkness of the storm cloud overhead, she said, "There was a strong sense of magnificent, awesome peace that fell over me." The peace was difficult to describe. There was no fear. There was no pain. She was acutely aware of exactly what was going on outside the darkened closet. She knew that the house was literally coming apart, piece by piece. She knew that there would not be much left judging by the intensity of the crashing and breaking she heard going on around her. She was aware that it was going to be very bad when she was able to get out. Pat was unaware of the eye passing overhead. She does not remember noticing a decrease or lull in the wind. The noises, crashing, and roaring started as soon as she got into the closet, and they kept going until the storm had passed.

As she was standing there, Pat noticed a 1-foot diameter hole in the sheetrock just above her head had opened. She was not aware of when the hole opened, nor did she know what impacted the wall to cause it. She just looked up and there it was.

There was no breeze that came through the hole, though she could see debris flying by in the sky above her. She could hear the noises outside but felt isolated and insulated by the beautiful feeling of peace that enveloped her.

Pat looked at her watch shortly after she got into the closet and again when the winds, rain, and hail stopped. It seemed like it took much longer, but only about 4 minutes had elapsed during the storm's fury and then it was quiet. After she was sure the storm had completely passed, Pat tried to open the closet door but was unable to do so. Large chunks of her house blocked the door. Pat was trapped and had no choice but to stand there in the tiny, sloped-ceiling closet and wait for help. That wonderful sense of peace was still present as she waited. Even though she was very aware of what happened outside, the calmness and peace lingered on. Pat knew she was going to be alright, and she knew she was going to be found.

She waited, standing in the dark, quiet, peaceful closet for almost an hour before she could hear the voices of people in front of the rubble of her home. She started yelling out, but they could not hear her and the voices went away. A short time later, she could hear voices outside again. She thought she heard her name and screamed out, "I am Pat! I am alive!" The voice outside belonged to her neighbor, Curtis.

Curtis yelled back to ask her where she was in the rubble. Pat knew there was a lot of damage but had no idea exactly how bad it was. She told him she was in a closet under the staircase. While she was standing there in the closet, she could hear Curtis make his way up the staircase above her to get a better view of the rubble of the house. Again, he asked where she was. Pat saw the hole in the sheetrock above her head and stuck her hand out from under the rubble right near his foot. Curtis and another man from the neighborhood started ripping pieces of the sheetrock away from around the hole to make it large enough for Pat to squeeze through. Both men took hold of Pat's arms and pulled her straight up out of the locked-in closet into the open air. As she balanced on a broken 2x4, there on the top of the stairway to nowhere, she found that she still had her cell phone in her pocket. Like most other cell phones in Joplin that night, it did not work, or at least, work very consistently.

The men were afraid the house might catch on fire because of the natural gas they could hear hissing from a broken pipe. With Pat freed from her small closet, the two men moved on down the street to assist others in the neighborhood. Pat had not smelled any gas while she was locked inside the closet. The downed power lines were crackling. The sense of peace was still present. She made it down through the huge piles of debris filling her front yard to the street below. It was cold and rainy. After both men left, the sense of peace diminished over the next 60 to 90 minutes before it was totally gone.

Pat looked around and saw her neighborhood was now dreary and ugly. The large trees were gone. The homes reduced to rubble. It was all gone. She felt as if she had been taken to a different time period. When she looked up at what was left of her home, all that remained was the staircase that went up to nothing and one interior wall that stood between the living quarters and the garage. The rest of the house was gone. She was not able to recover all the genealogy work she had researched. She was unable to find any of the letters her father had written to her mother in World War II. When she looked at what was left, she was not surprised that the people whose voices she heard while trapped in the closet did not stop to render aid. Pat would understand that, from the street, those people would likely have taken one look at what little was left of Pat's house and reasoned that there were realistically no survivors at that address and moved on. A lone staircase standing up in the rubble would not generally offer any hope to a rescue worker.

Pat and a neighbor walked to 26th Street, not too far from where she lived. She was trying to figure out what to do next as she just stood there on the corner. The son of one of her friends came to search for Pat and she was able to stay at their house for a short time. Her friends would drive her around for the next two weeks as she was still without a car. Pat lived in 5 different places over the next month.

When Pat looks back on that day, she knows God's angels were with her. The peace was just magnificent. She knows that God's grace was with her and feels tremendously blessed for what she experienced that day. Pat recognizes that the most important thing on earth now is life itself. She was able to volunteer through her church relief center to give back to the community that had reached out to help her in her time of need. She was able to bless many people with inspiration through her helping others when she had lost everything.

Pat had moved to Joplin about 11 months prior to the storm from Stillwater, Oklahoma and had had a conversation about her plans to downsides within the next two years with her daughters, Shannon and Kelly, and their families living in Oklahoma and Independence, Kansas. She had gotten rid of a few things since then, but now Pat says the Almighty took care of the rest. She went from a three-bedroom home before the storm, to a tiny, stairwell closet and one garage wall. Now, nearly everything she has is new. Several months later, when asked to give a testimony during church, Pat stood up and praised God that she was still the proud owner of her old washing machine and dryer which had been returned to her just a few weeks earlier.

◆ ◆ ◆

S cott and Judy had spent a good part of that Sunday afternoon enjoying their youngest son's graduation from Joplin High School held at Missouri Southern State University. After the ceremony was over and they had taken some pictures, they planned on meeting some of their family members for dinner at a restaurant on Range Line Road. While they were still at the ceremony site, the storm warning sirens sounded, causing them to change their plans.

Two golden retrievers waited for Scott and Judy in the back yard of their home near Irving Elementary School—Silas and Rowdy were both used in area hospitals as therapy dogs. Judy and Scott decided to make a short trip to their home to put the dogs inside the house. Over the past few years, Silas had developed a fear of thunderstorms and other loud noises; the dog was so unnerved by thunderstorms that he would claw to get into the house until his paws bled.

As they drove across town, they watched the sky grow dark. The rain had picked up considerably in the 10 minutes following graduation. The gusting winds were switching directions from one moment to the next. As Scott and Judy drove their tiny Scion, that Scott refers to as his "toaster," west on 20th Street near Delaware Avenue, Scott turned the radio on to see if there was a weather update. The first storm warning siren had stopped. The weather bulletin on the radio confirmed the sighting of a tornado near the intersection of 7th Street and Schifferdecker Avenue. The couple felt they were a safe distance away and could drive on to their house.

Scott, a self-described "storm nut," would often go out on the front porch and watch a storm blow through. He had taken some degree of enjoyment watching storms pass through as he was growing up. Scott had developed a pretty good sense of when he needed to get inside, away from an approaching storm. He grew up near Tulsa, Oklahoma and had been around tornadoes most of his life. He was not generally afraid of inclement weather, and the conditions did not look menacing enough to cause major concern.

As Scott pulled the tiny Scion to the intersection of

Connecticut Avenue and 20th Street, the weather report on the radio again announced a tornado was on the ground. There was fairly heavy rain and hail falling as they passed though the stoplight still headed west. Within a city block, the weather took a major turn for the worse. The car began jerking back and forth heavily in the buffeting winds. They were unaware of the massive storm closing in on them, now only about 6 blocks west. As they were approaching the Hampshire Terrace Apartments located just east of Dillons Grocery Store, Judy looked forward and asked what was ahead of them to the west. The sky was solid black and everything in it was moving sideways from left to right. Clouds were circling in the mossy-colored front face of the storm. Scott and Judy immediately realized they were driving into a tornado and had no escape route. The front wall of the storm near Joplin High School would be upon them within 30 seconds.

The car was near the corner of 20th Street and Vermont Avenue, in front of the Sew Neat shop. Scott decided to drive behind the shop to get out of the frontal force of the wind-driven hail and debris as best as he could. Time was running out. They knew they would have to stay in the car as there was no place nearby to seek shelter. The wind, coming out of the east, was hurling debris and hail at them. The car rocked heavily from side to side and Scott decided there might be more protection if he pulled the car around to the west side of the building. With no good place to hide on the west side of the store, Scott maneuvered the tiny car as close to the building as he could, facing the Hampshire Terrace Apartments across the street. The car was only a few inches from the wall and about 3 feet from the front corner of the building.

Scott had Judy duck her head down and he leaned over to try to cover her as best he could. Judy struggled because she had a firm grip on the passenger assist handle above the window and had no interest in letting go of it. The cramped quarters of the car did not afford Scott and Judy much place to hide. A few seconds after they had parked, the windows in the car blew out. Scott remembers the sudden drop in air pressure as his ears began to pop. It was louder than a jet engine and sounded nothing like a train. He would later describe a rhythmic whooshing sound. He could feel it in his ears as rain, hail, glass, wood, and other debris were pelting them. It had grown very dark under the dense shadow of the outer wall of the tornado.

Even amid the incredibly loud noise as the wind blew through the car, Scott could hear Judy praying. They were both praying for their children and families. The car rocked back and forth and up and down. They could feel the force of the wind and the car slightly lifting off the ground.

The noise, rain, and debris were intense as the couple huddled in the darkness. Both thought there was a reasonable chance they may not make it through alive. Just when they had all but given up, lights came on inside the car—the map reading lights located on the front ceiling of the car, near the inside rearview mirror. The small lights illuminated the darkness, filling the inside of the car. Scott had his eyes clinched tightly closed during the storm, but could see the illumination through his closed eyelids. The storm had not seemed to diminish at all. The brutal wind continued its assault. Judy felt that the onslaught of flying debris was never going to end. It kept coming.

When the winds and debris stopped, both Scott and Judy sat up and looked at each other to question what had happened with the lights. They both were acutely aware the lights came on. The lights had turned on simultaneously, but were governed individually by recessed, pushbuttons located just above the rearview mirror. There was no structural damage to the roof near the buttons. The debris that flew through the car during the storm could not have depressed both pushbutton switches at the same time. Adjacent to the map lights, the dome lamp that activates when the doors are opened was not on. It did not make any sense to either Scott or Judy how the lights could have possibly come on as they did. The intensity of the two small lights seemed extraordinarily bright and shattered the darkness.

When they were sure the storm had passed, Scott started up the car and edged it out from under a section of the Sew Neat shop roof that had come to rest on top of the car. Even though the car was filled with debris, the front seat area was relatively clear. There was an 8-foot-long piece of lumber stuck in the front of the car. One end was protruding through the grill and poked upwards through the middle of the hood. The other end was stuck through the middle of the shattered windshield, stopping inches away from Scott's head. There was another board that pierced the back of the Judy's seat. Nearly every house on the adjacent blocks was destroyed. The smell of natural gas filled the air. The still silence was soon replaced with calls for help. Both Scott and Judy would pick fiberglass, wood, asphalt, and all sorts of debris out of their skin and hair for 3 weeks following the storm.

After clearing out some of the debris from inside the car, they turned off the map lights and drove, now with two flat tires, west on 20th Street past Main Street. Scott parked the battered car and they walked to their house about a half-mile south, that had been in the center of the storm path. When they got to their home, there was not much left besides the hardwood floors. Rowdy, one of their golden retriever therapy dogs, did survive the storm.

Judy believes she and Scott survived the storm only by the grace of God and the power of an unseen hand that held them to the ground. They had a "cocoon" of protection she cannot explain. Had the car been 12 inches farther forward or back, the board piercing the hood would most likely have reached Scott or the board in Judy's seat would have reached her.

Scott says they were both at a very dark place in their lives during the storm, not only physically, but emotionally as well. They both thought they would not get out of the car alive. When the map lights illuminated simultaneously, an immediate sense of peace came over them. The thought of dying was instantly replaced by a strong sense of calm comfort. They believe the lights came on for a reason, encouraging them to hold on. It was their calm in the storm.

CHAPTER 21
HOPE

"A spirit glided past my face, and the hair on my body stood on end."—**Job 4:15 (NIV)**

"The lot is cast into the lap, but the decision is wholly of the Lord [even the events that seem accidental are really ordered by Him]."—**Proverbs 16:33 (AMPC)**

R ick was aware of the storm warnings in the Joplin area that Sunday afternoon, but the weather at the time seemed absolutely normal. Around 5 p.m. he received a call from his friend, Tommy, asking if he would go with him to Lowe's to pick up a new riding lawn tractor for Tommy's father. Rick hitched up a utility trailer to the back of his Suburban and headed to the store. He pulled his trailer to the front of the lawn and garden section where Tommy and his father were waiting for him with the new lawn tractor. Tommy and Rick were loading the new tractor onto the trailer when the first storm warning siren started sounding. Though Rick was aware of the potential for a severe storm, the siren caught him by surprise. Parked near the front of Lowe's, he could only see the sky to the east. He could not see the dark clouds forming to the south and west, behind the store.

The Lowe's employees had nearly finished securing the tractor to the trailer with straps when they told Rick they were heading into the store to heed the storm warning sirens, so Rick and Tommy finished securing the straps themselves. The men were trying to decide what to do next. Should they go into the store or try to make it home? The weather from where they were parked did not look that bad, but the store front stood between them and the telling clouds forming southwest of the city. They decided to go home and pulled out on Range Line Road, heading south. Tommy's father would go home in their car.

Rick and Tommy reached 32nd Street on Range Line Road and turned west toward Main Street. By the time they reached Main Street, the weather had become much more ominous, the sky to the west a black wall. There was no rain at the time and the wind had kicked up. Rick turned north on Main Street. Both were listening to the radio and checking the radar trying to figure out where the tornado was. They knew from the radio alerts that a tornado had touched down in Joplin. There were reports that it was north. There were reports that it was south. They really were not sure exactly where it was. By the time they reached 26th and Main Streets, the discussion between Rick and Tommy began to shift seriously toward where they should take cover, not if they should take cover. They had no idea a violent storm was beginning to organize in the southwest part of the city. They could see the huge black wall on the left side of the Suburban, but could not see any tornado, rotation, or debris.

By the time they got near 16th Street on Main Street, traffic came to a stop. There was a truck that blocked Main Street traffic while it backed a trailer with a "Rock Star Energy Drink" race boat into a parking lot between 15th and 16th Streets. Rick decided he could wait no longer and detoured right on 16th Street to Virginia Avenue. He then turned left to 15th Street and drove east toward Wal-Mart. As soon as Rick and Tommy turned east on 15th Street, they realized the weather was much more serious than they had initially thought. Tommy, sitting in the front passenger seat, could see blue flashes of transformers bursting to the south of them and slightly west. They raced down 15th Street toward Wal-Mart on a nearly empty street, with the trailer in tow.

Rick and Tommy were anxiously trying to figure out where

to take cover. For some reason, Rick had his mind set on Wal-Mart. Tommy kept telling Rick NOT to go to Wal-Mart for shelter. As they were going down 15th Street, they had to maneuver around several other cars hurrying to escape the path of the storm. Rick was overwhelmed with a feeling that they had to go to Wal-Mart. To Rick, there was no other option. He felt as if there was something in his head that kept saying, "Go there! Go there!" When they reached Range Line Road, the left turn lane was open, so Rick turned north and pulled through the parking lot of Burger King because he knew it was accessible to Wal-Mart. The sky to the west was nearly pitch black. The wind was gusting. The storm by now had devastated everything in its path halfway through the city and was a mile or so west of Wal-Mart. It was just minutes away.

Rick pulled the Suburban and trailer to the middle of the front of the store near the pharmacy entrance. He let Tommy out as close to the front door as he could. Tommy went into the store as Rick pulled the vehicle to the end of the pharmacy lane to park. As soon as Rick got out of the Suburban and locked the doors, he was hit with horizontal rain. He could hear the rumble of the storm quickly approaching from the west as he ran across the parking lot, but he would never look back. He knew the sound it was making was not normal. He already sensed it was there and it was not good. He was one of the last people to enter the store.

The employee locked the door behind Rick and told him to head to the designated safe areas near the back of the store where people already crowded several aisles. The lights inside the store were flickering on and off. By the time Rick reached the back of the store, where he would eventually ride the storm out, the storm was only about 30 seconds away, equivalent to a distance of about 3 blocks.

Hearing the noise of the storm and having seen the sky, Rick's heart grew heavy. He knew the storm was dangerous. He started to worry that there was a very good possibility he would not make it out alive. He began to think of his son, Shawn, and that he might not see him again. Rick looked at the bicycles hanging on the racks next to him and decided he did not want to take refuge in that aisle. Something inside told him there was a better place to be, so he moved to the next aisle over. He could hear some of the people grumbling and complaining as to why they were even there in the back of the store. He looked over and saw Tommy in one of the aisles near the bicycles as he passed by. Something in Rick's spirit told him he needed to be somewhere else and to keep moving. As Rick was excusing himself through the lines of people standing in the aisles near the back of the store, his mind was filled with thoughts of his son, Shawn. As a single father, Shawn was the most important thing to him. Shawn was all Rick had and he hoped he was safe, wherever he was. There was still something drawing Rick forward. He could not explain why. He had already passed by several aisles.

As Rick turned the corner down the next aisle, there was Shawn. He was standing with his mother, Kali, his step-father, and their son, Tristen. Rick did not know they were going to be there. Kali and her family had been at the Joplin High School graduation to watch her son Zach graduate, and had stopped at Wal-Mart on their way home—Zach had gone on to a friend's house in Carl Junction, Missouri after the graduation ceremony. Rick was able to tell Shawn he loved him. As soon as Rick saw Shawn, he had peace of mind knowing that the inner voice that pushed him through the store had led him to his son. He knew he could tell Shawn that they were going to make it through this storm in one piece.

Rick was wondering why everybody was still standing around as the storm closed in. He screamed for everybody to get down on the floor. As they got down, Rick would tell Shawn it was just like they practiced in school; "Get down and cover yourself the best you can." Rick lay down over the top of Shawn to protect his son, while Kali's husband took care of her and Tristen. The noises outside intensified as the storm made its way across the parking lot toward the front of the store. Rick held onto Shawn with one hand and a shopping cart lying on the floor next to him with the other. He thought that if the shopping cart began to move around too much or start flying, he would just let go of it, but at the time, there was nothing else for Rick to hold on to.

The remainder of the lights had gone off as the noises outside increased. The ceiling tiles heaved as the front of the store was slammed by the front wall of the storm. The roof peeled away. The noise was intense as metal twisted and glass shattered. There were loud crashes and explosions that rocked the areas all around them. Rick knew the front of the store was severely damaged as he could feel the wind and rain on his back. The amount of rain and the force of the wind driving it was comparable to that of a pressure washer.

Rick could feel the eye of the storm as it passed overhead; there was a "whooshing" sound as it made its way across the battered building. Some people thought it was over. Rick told them to stay down as there was probably more to come. The lightning and thunder were unlike anything he had ever seen or heard before.

When Tommy had reached an area near the toys toward the back of the store, he met a grandmother with her 3-month-old grandson, Grayson, in a car seat. She asked Tommy if he could help protect the baby. Tommy lay over the child, still strapped in his car seat, as the storm ravaged the building. The force of the powerful wind pushed Tommy, laying over Grayson's car seat, around in the aisle while the debris continued falling on top of them. Tommy was worried that he and Grayson might be pulled out of the building by the powerful winds. He was praying God would protect them in that moment. A shelf full of games and toys fell onto Tommy's back, pinning him and Grayson to the floor. Grayson escaped without any serious injuries as Tommy had shielded him.

Shawn and Rick were able to make it through the storm safely; as did Kali, her husband, and their son. There was the strong smell of natural gas in the debris-filled store after the winds blew through.

There were about 15 to 20 people who worked together to get out of the debris piles that filled every aisle of the wrecked store. Rick was able to get to where Tommy and Grayson were buried in the debris and help them out. The group of people managed to forge their way toward the front of the store and reach the safety of the parking lot about an hour later.

Rick had been slipping on the water-covered floor in the flip-flops he wore and thought he would go to his Suburban parked out in front of the store and get the pair of shoes that were there. He walked to where he had parked. The once new lawn tractor was nearby, beaten up and smashed by the storm —he would locate the demolished Suburban the next day, but the trailer would never be found. Rick could see the battered St. John's Hospital on the horizon across town. The devastation of the storm began to sink in.

Looking back, Rick can't explain how he was guided to Wal-Mart. He just was. There were many opportunities presented for him to take a route that would have led him away from the storm's path. Had the "Rock Star Energy Drink" race boat not been blocking Main Street, he would have continued north. He believes he was just steered toward that location and was guided back through the individual aisles to get to his son's side. There was no peace within him until he reached his son.

Had they taken any one of those turns to get out of the path of the storm, Tommy would not have been in position to protect Grayson in the car seat. If Tommy was not there, would somebody else have been present to take that role? There are so many things that could have turned out differently with possible tragic results with just one detour.

"It was the grace of God that directed me to that store," Rick said. He has no other realistic explanation. Rick ignored his inclinations and followed the voice saying, "Do this! Do this! Do this!"

God led—and Rick followed.

CHAPTER 22
THE ANGELS CAME

"Then suddenly there appeared with the angel an army of the troops of heaven (a heavenly knighthood), praising God and saying, Glory to God in the highest [heaven], and on earth peace among men with whom He is well pleased [men of goodwill, of His favor]."—**Luke 2:13-14 (AMPC)**

"He had a dream in which he saw a stairway resting on the earth, with its top reaching to heaven, and the angels of God were ascending and descending on it."—**Genesis 28:12 (NIV)**

T he storm left its indelible mark on the city that Sunday afternoon—May 22, 2011. Joplin, Missouri had taken a direct hit from what would end up being the 7th largest single tornado in national history. The last time such a devastating tornado had hit the United States was in 1947. The nearly mile-wide storm cut a swath directly through the middle of the city, obliterating nearly everything in its path. At one point, near the middle of Joplin, the width of the storm damaged area was approximately 2 miles wide, stretching from 7th Street on the northernmost edge, all the way to 31st Street on the southern edge. For all practical purposes, the middle third of the city was gone. The old postal lines of zip codes north or south of 15th Street would now be changed to reference the path of the storm. People of Joplin would reference where they live or where they were at the time of the storm to their proximity to the destruction. "The Zone," as referred to by the Joplin Area Chamber of Commerce, would be the new reference point for the people of Joplin.

The dawn of the next day was the first opportunity for the people of Joplin to see what they had survived. Electrical and phone lines were a tangled mess throughout the city. Power was out for most of the city. Communication was only possible through sporadic cell service. The weather went back and forth between stormy or sunny, depending on the time of day.

Jackie was in her home near Connecticut Avenue late in the morning on Monday, May 23rd. The electrical power to her house was still out. Her home was far enough away from the path of the storm that there had been only moderate damage. She would need some new windows and shingles and had a fair amount of debris in her yard, but for the most part, her house was livable compared to the total destruction only 2 blocks away. The next-door neighbor's fence had been blown down by the storm winds, leaving a wide-open expanse behind her home.

As she sat in her recliner, looking out the windows at the rear of her house, she saw a group of five people walking on the elevated railroad track bed 200 feet behind her home. They were all wearing white clothes. They looked like a family. Some were taller than others. Her first thought was that they were probably from the area on the other side of the tracks were there had been considerable damage to homes and businesses. She felt empathetic. Perhaps, they had lost everything, and somebody gave them the long, white T-shirts to wear as their own clothes were lost in the storm?

As Jackie watched from her living room, she noticed the group of people in long, white T-shirts begin to walk down the embankment from the tracks toward her home. They walked down the hill side by side in some semblance of a row, stretching 15 feet from one end to another. Surprisingly, more people in white immediately came into view behind them. They seemed to be coming up from the other side of the raised railroad bed. There were twice as many people in this second row, stretching over 20 feet in length. Jackie began to realize this was not a family, as there were too many people. This had to be something else.

As Jackie continued to watch, she saw the second row descend the hill as a third row of people in white appeared. There were more than 20 people in that row, stretching about 40 feet in length. The front rows continued to advance toward Jackie, still seated in her living room. As they approached, she was able to distinguish more detail of the individual people. She could see that the clothes were not T-shirts. They were wearing full-length white flowing robes. The garments were clean and spotless. They were all dressed identically. She could not distinguish detail in their faces. It was as if there was just a polished bronze surface where the faces should have been. Jackie felt a strong sense of peace. She did not feel confused or threatened in any manner.

"These must be angels," Jackie said to herself.

The third row of angels was followed immediately by a fourth row, longer than the third. The fourth row was followed by another, and another, and another. Each row incrementally longer than the previous row. The angels in the flowing, clean, white, spotless robes just kept coming over that hill, seemingly from the other side of the railroad track bed. It was like a large wave washing over a wall, starting first in a trickle, and then steadily increasing to a sea of white. There was a fifth row, and a sixth row, and a seventh row, and on, and on, and on. They just kept coming.

The wave was getting closer and closer to where Jackie was sitting, row by row. Soon, they were within a few feet of her window when the first row came to a stop. As the angels in front halted, the back rows were still coming over the hill by the tracks. Those in the back rows continued to advance down the hill and fall into rank. Before long, the hillside was covered and the army of white-robed angels stretched into the horizon. The flow did not stop when the hillside was covered. As Jackie watched, the open sky above the top row standing on the railroad track bed began to fill up as well. The horizon grew taller. The advancing rows stopped, but the flow continued, pushing forward. They appeared to stack on top of each other. This continued until the entire view through Jackie's window was filled with a multitude of white-robed angels. They stretched as far as she could see from left to right and filled the vertical limits of the window as well. "There were hundreds and hundreds, or a thousand, or more," Jackie said.

"Why are they stopping," she wondered. A voice from her left side answered, "Let us pray as Jesus taught us to pray." The angels began to pray. Jackie closed her eyes as they all prayed the Lord's Prayer.

"Our Father Who is in Heaven, hallowed be Your Name. Your Kingdom come. Your will be done on earth as it is in Heaven. Give us day by day our daily bread. And forgive us our sins, for we also forgive everyone who is indebted to us. And do not lead us into temptation, but deliver us from the evil one."

On her right side, Jackie could feel the presence of the Holy Spirit. When she finished praying the Lord's Prayer with the angels, she opened her eyes, and the multitude of white-robed angels were gone.

"Bless the Lord, you His angels, mighty in strength,
who perform His Word, obeying the voice of His Word!
Bless the Lord, all you His angels, you who serve Him,
doing His will."—Psalm 103:20-21 (NASV)

He sent the angels...

and the angels came.

CHAPTER 23
SHORTAGE OF TIME

I t is 5:38 p.m., Sunday, May 22, 2011. "I have so much on my mind. It is a Sunday afternoon and I have all kinds of plans. There is a threat of bad weather in the area, but it will most likely happen somewhere else. It never happens here. It always happens somewhere else. There is no need to worry about anything. This storm, like so many others have done in the past, will probably go away. If it doesn't go away, it will probably miss me. If it does actually end up coming near me, I will be alright. How bad can it be? They hardly ever materialize. There are so many false alarms. Why should this alarm matter now? Why is this storm any different?"

Now step ahead just a few minutes and ask yourself those same questions. Use the same reasoning. This storm would truly be different from the others. This storm changed the lives of many people. In just a matter of 20 minutes, the heart of Joplin, Missouri had been significantly damaged or demolished. This storm was not selective. It destroyed nearly everything in its path. On a smaller scale, it traveled the city 1 block at a time—destroying 6 to 10 city blocks every 10 seconds. It did not care if you were rich or poor. It did not care if you were young or old. It did not care if you were married or single. It did not care if you were in your car, at a business, or in your home. If you were in the middle one-third of the city on May 22, 2011, your life was going to be dramatically changed. You might make it through with only a few scratches and cuts. For some, life would end.

The storm left us with questions that cannot be answered with our limited intelligence or reasoning. A question will not always lead us to understanding. More often than not, it just leads us to another question that we still can't answer. Why was one person taken while those on either side of them spared? Why me? Why my family? Why not some other family? Why did it have to happen this way? Why not me instead of them?

Why?

One question just leads us to another question.

I did not lose any family members due to this storm. I cannot imagine the grief that goes with losing a parent, or worse, a child; much less multiple children or a family. I did not suffer the experience of digging through the shattered remains of my hopes and dreams—trying to fill up a shoebox with broken pieces of my past. I cannot fathom the heart-wrenching feeling that is present when life and property are lost. I just cannot imagine what it was really like for those families.

As I stated previously, I do not profess to have the answers. I do firmly believe that, in time, we will know and understand the answers fully.

Most of the people interviewed for this book had several things in common. Some similarities were noted as the storm approached. Other similarities were noticed after the storm had long been gone...

1. When they realized the storm was inevitable, the reaction time was very limited. Almost all of the people had 30 seconds or less to prepare. Most had less than 10 seconds to make important decisions. Some had no time at all to think about their choices. They were unaware of the storm outside, until they were included in its fury. There was no time to prepare. Their lives were where they were, and they were not going to be anything different. There just would not be enough time.

2. Even amid the raging noise and chaos as their surroundings disintegrated around them, they all had a sense of incredible peace. They had acceptance of how it could end up. They may not make it through the destruction, but there was peace. There was, for the most part, acceptance of the finality of their situation. No matter what, there was nothing they could do to change things. They were where they were, and that was that.

3. They all prayed to God. Some of them offered up very detailed prayers. Some asked for deliverance from the storm, or for the safety of their children and families. Others offered praises and thanksgiving for God's presence in the storm. Some simply called out the name of Jesus. They all prayed to God.

4. For the people we interviewed, almost all were very thankful they had survived. Some described being given a second chance to make a difference in other people's lives. Some gave back to the community that helped them. Almost all recognize they were truly given another chance to make necessary changes in their lives. Nearly all have drawn spiritually closer to God in their personal and family lives. Most recognize they have different priorities now and they are different people than they were on May 21, 2011.

5. Things, even the family heirlooms, are not as important as they once thought. It is difficult to place too much emphasis or dwell on the loss of the material items in your life when they are gone, probably somewhere between Joplin and Springfield or beyond, or in a landfill, and they are not very likely to ever

come back. Almost all the people we interviewed now place a higher value on the non-material things. A woman named Carolyn once told me she had an ugly blue tarp over her house, but it didn't matter. All the other homes that remained standing in her neighborhood also had one. She just has her huggables —her family—and that is enough. Another woman, Tina, says her family does far more together. Where her children used to spend a lot of time with their friends on the computer or phone, now they spend more time as a family. "Stuff" really is "stuff." Priorities have changed.

6. The people who lost their lives due to the storm that day were not bad people deserving punishment or wrath. None of the people interviewed for this book look down on those individuals or families who lost family members. This storm is the twine that binds them all together. They don't consider themselves any more special just because they were spared. Their lives are not more important than those people who were lost that day. None of them claim to be superior or perfect by any measure. They all admit they have plenty of room to improve. They don't consider themselves lucky. Not one of them even used the word "lucky" in the interviews. Most of them consider themselves blessed. They all recognize that survival of the storm was not a rite of passage in itself. They are not guaranteed a tomorrow or the next day. If it is God's will, they will not make it through even one more day.

7. They all recognize the frailty of life. Most think about their future more seriously. Many of them are acutely aware of where they are spiritually. Many of them recognize they are much farther down the road spiritually than before the storm. They seem intent on not going back to where they were. They are all aware of God. They may address Him as "the Good Lord," or a "Higher Power," or other names, but they all refer to God. They recognize the need for God to be in their lives personally, on a daily basis.

This last item on the list above was not based on any particular Christian denomination. It is based more on their understanding and personal experiences. Looking at the broad basics of salvation according to different denominations of Western Christian religions, you can see some of the differences, but there are definite similarities among them. The doctrines that historically have been affirmed by Catholic, Orthodox, most Protestant, and Western Christian religions start on the premise that you: 1) Acknowledge that we, as human beings, are sinners and ask Jesus for forgiveness for our sins, and repent, or turn back from our sinful nature; 2) That Jesus came to this earth, suffered, died on the cross, and was buried for our sins; 3) That Jesus rose from the grave defeating death, that we may be pardoned and receive forgiveness for our sins; 4) That God saves us by His merciful grace.

Some Christian denominations enlist the use of "The Sinner's Prayer" to simplify those steps. It really is a simple, straightforward prayer. Some of the Western religious denominations go a bit further and add the need for the display of works to show the intent of the heart, or other steps. The purpose here is not to debate or dispute which denomination is right. It is not to condemn the doctrine of one Christian group over another. The purpose is to draw to the point that the basic requirements, as found in "The Sinner's Prayer," are still very similar: admit that you are a sinner and ask Jesus to forgive you; repent or turn back from your sins; acknowledge that Jesus came to this earth, suffered, died on the cross, and was buried for your sins; acknowledge that Jesus rose from the grave defeating death, so you may receive forgiveness for your sins through His mercy and grace. When you decide to start, and pray the "Sinner's Prayer," or a "Confession of Faith," you see that this initial step only takes only about 15 to 20 seconds to get through. This crucial step may help initiate, define, or redefine future events that lie ahead for you.

As it is written in Romans 10:13, *"Call on the Name of the Lord and you will be saved."* This says we will be saved, not safe. "Saved" refers to an eternal state. "Safety" from a storm is temporary. Being "saved" does not guarantee your body will survive a severe storm. It is much bigger than just a severe storm.

Now go back to the first paragraph of this chapter and look at the questions at the end of paragraph. Go ahead and put in the answers as you know them. Events can be very hard, and they were on May 22, 2011. The alarm was telling that a severe storm was on its way and it was true. This storm was different because you may now be given another chance to make some crucial decisions and corrections in your life. The first step only takes about 15 to 20 seconds to get through. You read stories here about many people who were confronted with the fury of reality and had much less time to react. Even those who had the full 30 seconds to prepare had a lot more on their minds than going through a 15-second "Confession of Faith."

Imagine it is now 5:40 p.m. Sunday, May 22, 2011 and counting.

The time is now. Do not delay.

Your life may be forever altered in the next 60 seconds.

What decision are you going to make?

...PRAISE GOD!

ACKNOWLEDGEMENT

I would like to extend a special thank you to the following persons:

Shannon Duhon, and his wife, Krista, who graciously agreed to deplete every red pen in their household and surely make numerous trips to Office Depot to get more. They agreed to correct my grammatical errors and draw many, pretty red marks through words "that" were not needed. Some of the pages would have been more easily edited by just spray painting them red. Thank you, Shannon and Krista.

I want to extend a special thank you to Jeris Joyner and Katelyn Rae for their expertise, input, and direction. Their work allowed this project to be taken from its long-time resting place on the shelf through narrow prepublication deadlines and guide it to completion. This task would be formidable for me, without them. Thank you both so much for being such a blessing.

Thank you also, to the following individuals for their input in completing this project: George, Max, Isaac, Jennifer, Carter, Donna, and William.

ABOUT THE AUTHOR

Dr. Larry Brothers

Dr. Larry Brothers is a lifelong resident of Joplin, Missouri. He has been married to Rosie for 36 years; they have one son Dalton, and daughter-in-law, Christa.

Dr. Brothers works as an optometrist in a family-established multi-doctor practice. His father and brother both retired from the business and Dalton is now in practice with him. Larry and Rosie are the proud grandparents of three beautiful granddaughters.